CW01500207

Christopher Webber

GET THE ELEPHANT OUT OF THE ROOM:

A GUIDE TO OUTSMARTING DIFFICULT PEOPLE AT WORK

Christopher Webber

www.foxleigh.net

Published by Foxleigh Consulting Ltd

ISBN 978-1-0684918-1-8

SECTION 01: PEOPLE, THE POWER BEHIND SUCCESSFUL ORGANISATIONS

SECTION 02: DIFFICULT COLLEAGUES

SECTION 03: DIFFICULT MANAGERS

SECTION 04: DIFFICULT CUSTOMERS

SECTION 05: HOW TO SUCCEED

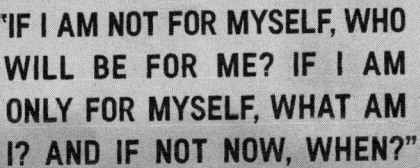

"IF I AM NOT FOR MYSELF, WHO WILL BE FOR ME? IF I AM ONLY FOR MYSELF, WHAT AM I? AND IF NOT NOW, WHEN?"

—Rabbi Hillel

GETTING A COMMERCIAL EDGE

When I was a young salesperson learning my trade as a primary and secondary care sales representative in South Wales, I encountered a customer who was an incredible challenge. This customer haunted me for several years and was a source of intense frustration.

I did not understand his actions or behaviour, or why he refused to listen to me and my arguments.

This was my first significant experience of this kind of resistance, and over the years since, I have used it as a source of personal reflection and growth.

I have revisited the challenge and used it as a barometer of my development. I asked myself, what would I do if I came across this customer now? The answer I came up with told me much about how far I have come and the lessons I have learned.

At the time, I was desperate to prove myself in a new career and find a new direction in life. It was the most essential thing in the world at that moment, and I could not accept failure.

When I encountered this customer, I believed he conspired against me to make my life impossible and block my progress.

Since then, I have encountered others, customers, colleagues, managers, and equally challenging partners. During each, I encountered significant frustrations and emotional barriers, but my career evolved and developed to the point where dealing with and succeeding despite these people became my hallmark.

So, where did it all start, and how was this talent for overcoming difficult people born?

It was during my first full-time job as a dedicated salesperson for Sanofi Synthelabo in 1999.

My job was as a sales representative in South East Wales, promoting three products to general practice and hospitals in the region. We sold a product for blood pressure, a treatment for benign prostate disease and a painkiller.

I worked with a territory partner, an experienced salesperson called Graeme Doherty, someone from whom I learned much early in my career and whose words of advice still echo in my ears 25 years later.

The challenge I faced was to convince a urology surgeon at The Royal Glamorgan Hospital to use our prostate disease drug in his patients.

At that time, the Royal Glamorgan Hospital was new, just west of Cardiff, serving some of the more deprived areas of the South Wales valleys.

The surgeon was one of six or seven in Eastern Wales working in urology, which perhaps passed me by at the time because it indicates something of the competitive world in which he worked.

Surgeons spend many years learning and perfecting their craft. Through years of practice, they develop incredible, delicate fine motor skills. They work to repair delicate tissues, remove growths, and clear debris so that our bodies can function somewhat normally again.

Surgery is a revered skill, and consultant surgeons are some of the most widely respected doctors worldwide because of their deft skills.

With this backdrop, I enter a young, enthusiastic salesperson desperate to make an impression.

I had moved to South Wales as a restart to my life. I had spent all my previous life living in St Helens, a small town between Liverpool and Manchester.

St Helens, a former industrial town home to world-class businesses such as Pilkington's Glass and Beechams, struggled to recover in the early 1980s.

Unemployment was common, and for many, the prospect of a job with a monthly salary was a dream when most people worked in jobs that paid a weekly cash wage.

As a child, I was obsessed with sports. My dream was to be at the Olympic Games or to play in front of thousands of people in a Rugby League Cup Final at Wembley or Old Trafford.

St Helens is famous for its Rugby League team, and the sport is almost a religion in the town.

I thought my dreams had come true when I signed a professional rugby league contract with arch-rivals Wigan in 1995. At the time, they were the most professional club in the country and dominated the sport.

I was excited to embark on my sporting career with them, and from the first moment, I found myself mixing with game legends during training sessions. I was training with the Great Britain captain, sharing a weights room with stars of the day and of the future, and I was part of a club that was transforming how the sport was played and coached.

However, my dreams fell apart three years later when I was told that I was not big enough or developing fast enough to be part of the first team squad long term, and my contract was cancelled.

I remember feeling intense loss in a corridor under the main stand. I lost my dreams, but I also had a personal sense of being lost.

It felt as if my world had ended.

I desperately needed a way to build a future, and sales was my way.

A few months later, I sat in a pub and realised that if I could sell, there would always be a job because people would always need to buy products and services.

I was fortunate enough to find a job as a contract salesperson for a pharmaceutical company working across Manchester and Cheshire, and my new journey began.

A year later, I moved to South Wales to reinvent myself, build a future and a family and start again. That is when I found myself challenged by the problem of the urology surgeon at The Royal Glamorgan Hospital.

The problem was that he refused to use my product and instead prescribed the leading competitor brand.

This was a significant problem because hospital doctors have a substantial influence. They are rightly respected as experts in their field, and their choices are mirrored by the choices of junior hospital staff and general practitioners in the community.

This one consultant surgeon's decision to use our competition significantly thwarted our goal of growing our product sales in the area.

It became a key objective of mine to influence this particular consultant to change his mind and choose our product.

I was not the first to face this challenge. I followed another representative onto the territory. He was widely respected inside and outside the company and faced the same difficulty growing his sales.

He had moved on, reputation intact, but had failed to change the surgeon's mind.

I was determined to be different and could change his mind, and I set out to make it happen.

The first step was to book an appointment with him through his secretary.

I walked into the new office within the brand-new hospital building one Tuesday afternoon to book an appointment.

I talked to his secretary, a warm, engaging and fascinating woman in her mid-forties. We got along very well, and I learned that she was friendly towards me, which is not always the case. Often, secretaries are instructed to be the defenders of the diary, and they protect the time of their consultant with vigour and commitment, refusing appointments flatly.

This did not happen in this case, but she did refuse to book an appointment.

She knew my company, my intention, and her boss's position. He preferred to use my competitor's brand, and there was no point in wasting my time and his time arranging a pointless meeting.

I was heartbroken, but I did not give up and continued to call into the hospital to meet with him, his team, and his colleagues. What choice did I have? It was my job, and this was one of the most significant barriers to my success.

If I were going to make anything of my new direction in life, I needed to navigate this challenge and succeed.

One afternoon, while I was in the office trying to talk to a team member, the surgeon walked in.

This was my moment!

Persistence, effort, charm, and luck came together, and I had the chance to talk to the man who presented the most significant opportunity to prove myself.

I plucked up the courage, and I introduced myself and my company.

He was polite and responded to my greeting.

I told him why I was there and wanted to discuss my product.

His reaction provided me with the gold that I was seeking. At that moment, I heard something I believed would change everything and open the door to transformation.

He told me that he preferred the other product because it was a once-per-day treatment, whilst ours was a twice-daily drug.

He said, "Come back and see me when you have a once-per-day treatment."

I thought I had unlocked the secret and was about to discover treasure because I knew, at that time, that in the pipeline of development was a once-per-day version of our drug.

I was excited.

I could not say anything at the time because of the strict rules on promotion surrounding medicines, but I was ready and excited for the moment when I could finally change his mind.

The day came about 9 months later.

Our once-daily treatment was finally available on the market, and I could proactively discuss it with customers. Of course, I headed to The Royal Glamorgan Hospital to meet with the doctor who had held the keys to my future success.

For the second time, fortune smiled at me, or so I thought, because when I walked into his secretary's office, he was standing there.

This was my moment.

As I stood in the doorway, I told him, "You told me to come back when I had a once-per-day version; well, it is here, and so am I."

I asked him to sit with me while I discussed the product details and his views.

He flatly refused.

I couldn't believe it.

I was furious!

"What!" I exclaimed. "But you said…"

"I know what I said", he responded coolly, "but I am not interested."

I don't remember what happened next, but I remember how I felt. Anger burned inside me, a rage fueled by the unfairness of life as I saw it.

How dare he respond like that! Had he lied to me?

He asked for once per day, and here I was, as requested, delivering just the product he wanted.

I turned on my heels, stormed out of the office and slammed the door, never to return.

That moment has followed me for many years.

Within that series of events with that particular customer are many lessons in sales, relationship management, self-control, strategy, and dealing with difficult customers.

I have often used that challenge to help me understand the problems we face with difficult customers and, indeed, difficult people at work.

That moment has inspired my life's work, laid the foundation for my business, and inspired this book.

In the years since that day, I have discovered some truths about demanding customers. These truths have become central to success despite these difficulties and are contained within this book.

In the years since that day, many client engagements started with the phrase, "We have a problem with…" before my client went on to explain their challenges.

These words inspired Foxleigh and our mission to help clients succeed with even difficult customers.

The founding insight that enables us to solve client problems regardless of how difficult the customer is is that most people do not set out to be difficult, no matter what they say or do.

They are not sitting in their office working out plans to block our progress and dash our dreams.

It does not matter if they are customers, colleagues within our organisation, leaders, or managers; their focus is almost unwavering on their success.

They are dedicated to their progress.

They might need to block your ideas, reject your proposals, or oppose you to achieve their success, but they are far more likely to be chasing their dreams than trying to stop you from achieving yours.

When I think about the intentions of that surgeon all those years ago, I am convinced that he had no personal crusade against my product.

As I thought, he was not so committed to the alternative brand that he could not change his mind.

Neither product was important enough for him to care.

He was, first and foremost, a surgeon who had dedicated much of his life to learning to perfect his craft.

The use of pharmaceuticals was not part of that identity. It was the opposite. If the use of drugs could cure patients, what was his function?

His use of medicines was probably a necessity. Any reasonable medic should accept it as part of patient care and deliver value-for-money care.

He chose a brand because it was needed. But I expect that if tested, he cared little about the one he decided on, other than that it was the most suitable at the moment he decided it.

He used medication as a tool, but his true passion was his skill to use his strength, which is his delicate hand, as a surgeon.

He was not being difficult. He was pragmatic, and it was my problem that I failed to see. I also failed to be creative and flexible enough to work through the challenges he created.

My mission today is to help others understand the motives of their difficult customers or the difficult people at work.

This book is dedicated to sharing their motives and allowing you to understand them. We share what could be driving their actions, decode their thinking, and enable you to progress by adapting, learning, and thinking to resolve these challenges so that you can succeed.

There are no easy answers for difficult customers and people. They see the world differently from us and are interested in their success. But by recognising that we first must know the world as we see it to find solutions, we challenge ourselves to think in new ways.

We can unlock partnerships that seemed impossible by solving the problems they are trying to solve.

By stepping away from our perspective, we broaden our horizons and find new ways to progress.

Sometimes, we need to accept that if we are to succeed with these people, we must change, and then we have a choice.

How important is it that we succeed here? We must ask ourselves.

If it is essential, we must change and adapt. If it is not crucial, we can choose not to change and accept that we will never resolve the problem.

Whatever the choice, a deeper understanding of why it was difficult will unlock logic and ideas in our brains and keep our emotions in check, which is the basis for resolution.

As we will see, emotions can be our enemies, and every new solution starts with learning to see beyond them.

I have spent the last 25 years of my career developing, evolving, and honing my skills for succeeding with difficult people.

As a teacher and adviser, it has become my business to understand, solve, and help my clients adapt to the challenges of demanding customers, partners, and colleagues.

I teach the skills of understanding and empathy. I help clients explore the emotions that drive others' behaviours and create their reactions. I enable them to plan ways to use this understanding to improve their position, build trust, and succeed.

This book explores difficult people at work in various forms. We unpick their behaviours, suggest why they might act in specific ways, and provide ideas and strategies to help you succeed.

The book is divided into sections. We will explore difficult colleagues, managers, and customers. We will also examine examples of different personalities within each group and how they behave, trying to understand their motives and intentions before sharing ideas on how to succeed with each personality type.

The final section is explicitly designed with tools and techniques to help us better understand why people soem difficult, where the problems are, and how to adapt and change to achieve more.

Getting the olephant out of the room means that you need to see that it is there, and then you need to change. Notlcing tho problem creates responsibility for solving it, and because you are the one to see the issue, you are the one who must adapt.

You don't need to compromise your mission, but you do need to be prepared to detour in order to accommodate someone who is important and who, without your ability to change, will be a significant barrier.

In this book, we will explore the people, their motives, and offer you insight into what you need to do to adapt and overcome barriers.

Difficult people are everywhere. Learning to succeed despite them transforms people from ordinary to extraordinary, reduces personal stress, and builds partnerships that have become a source of pride and value for many years.

But first, let's explain why people are so important for excellence long term. In the next section, we will share examples of when people have made a huge difference to results and when failing to empower them or failing to overcome difficulties has led to disaster.

SECTION 01:
PEOPLE, THE POWER BEHIND SUCCESSFUL ORGANISATIONS

FROM GOOD TO GREAT

One afternoon in 2015, I was walking through Berkhamsted. It was cold and grey, and I arrived at my hotel earlier than usual after a client meeting.

Berkhamsted is a small town a few miles north of London. It is populated by bankers, lawyers and business people who crave the countryside but must be within a commutable distance of London and their offices.

It is a relatively wealthy area with a healthy shopping street and various shops, restaurants, and cafes.

That afternoon, the street was quiet, perhaps because of the cold. I was wrapped in a warm coat and scarf, dashing between the railway station at the bottom of the hill and my hotel at the end of the line of shops.

At the time, I worked as a consultant for a negotiation company. I spent a lot of time in hotels running training events, supporting clients with commercial advice and helping groups and individuals with their negotiation planning.

It was my job to be a negotiation expert, something that I took great pride in, but my role was more significant than that. An expert in negotiation in isolation seemed limited in value, and I wanted to bring as much as possible to delight my clients.

They were running businesses faced with negotiation challenges and, by the nature of my role, were seeking to take business performance to a higher level. They wanted someone who knew about negotiation but also learned about business, someone who could advise them on negotiation strategy in the context of business, tailor advice, and connect ideas directly to their aspirations.

This was a challenge to build my knowledge and enrich my meetings with them, using a broad base of insight and experience. I recognised that I needed to be well-read, thoughtful, credible, and confident in my business acumen to stand out.

I had spent the previous year or two immersed in negotiation, reading books and talking to experts about the nuances of behaviour, tactics and strategy. It was time to expand my base.

I had time to myself that grey afternoon, and as I strolled back towards my hotel at the end of the day, an Oxfam shop caught my eye.

It was a second-hand bookshop, and unlike many charity shops, it was neatly arranged and organised.

My eyes lit up as I saw the business section and was drawn inside.

I came across an almost pristine copy of Good to Great by Jim Collins, and I picked it up immediately.

This is an infamous book built on the research of Jim and his colleagues, who were set on understanding how some companies leap from being good companies that perform well to great companies that are outstanding in their field.

I took it back to my hotel and immediately found myself immersed in it.

That evening, as I walked to a local restaurant to eat, I carried the book with me to read at the table while I waited for my food.

That evening and for many evenings that followed, I read the ideas intently, looking up only to fork a mouthful of food into my mouth or to sip my pint of beer.

As I read the book, I was struck by some captivating ideas about how these businesses transformed their performance.

FIRST, WHO, THEN WHAT

In the book, Jim cites examples such as Hewlett-Packard, which, when founded in 1937, set out to manufacture electronic devices but was not specific about which devices it would manufacture.

Their initial mission was to build a team of people they would trust to make the company around—a core of ultra-talented individuals who would become greater than the sum of their parts and contribute to its success.

After the Second World War, revenue from government contracts declined, so they doubled down on recruiting talent.

Counter to the instincts of many executives today, as revenues were falling, Hewlett-Packard stepped up their recruitment of recently available scientists after leaving government laboratories.

They committed to finding the talent they could use to create the products that would set them apart.

They understood that the team inside the business would create the products needed to succeed in the markets they entered and develop the culture in which the whole company would thrive.

It is essential to understand what makes companies successful. Is it the people working there or the products and services they create and sell?

If a company has created an incredible product comprised of people who struggle to work productively together, will the company thrive?

The answer is that wonderful products can only take an organisation so far, but the team must also be strong to fully benefit from brilliant products.

The same is equally valid: Organisations that sell products similar to the competition can gain an advantage through the strength of their people.

Patagonia is an outdoor clothing company based in California, US.

They operate in a highly competitive market, selling clothing for people who hike, ski, snowboard, camp, climb, and explore the world's wilds.

They have dozens of competitors on the market, and many of them have created innovative fabrics and a diverse portfolio at various price points, all in an attempt to build success.

However, Patagonia has a reputation as one of the strongest brands in the sector and within the much larger clothing segment.

Dean Carter, a stocky, fit-looking man with grey hair and stubble, joined Patagonia in 2015 as the Chief People Officer.

Like many at the company, he enjoyed the outdoors, including hiking, snowboarding, and swimming. In an interview, he said that when he joined the team, he committed to swimming more after he moved to California to take on the role.

During his tenure, Dean brought to life the power of people in the organisation and implemented some unique, innovative, and ultimately compelling policies.

His focus was recruiting, retaining, and crucially nurturing the best talent in the industry, something he knew would be a critical driver in company performance.

His policies, including providing company-paid nannies to female executives on business trips so they could be with their children and be fully productive, had an enormous impact on retention.

They retained 100% of female staff after they had children, which is unheard of in almost any industry.

In 2019, Patagonia's people turnover was around 4% per year, compared to over 15% in the broader industry, a testament to the atmosphere created in the business.

Patagonia's mission is clear: protect the environment. They live this mission and celebrate employees who do the same.

They encourage staff to ski when powder is on the slopes and surf when the waves are right. They also recruit climate activists and encourage them to continue with peaceful protesting.

Patagonia operates in a highly competitive marketplace, with few easy opportunities to differentiate based on products alone.

They have a reputation for creating quality garments, being ethical, and protecting the world in which they want their customers to enjoy.

This combination of a clear mission and the level of focus and importance placed on their teams by people like Dean Carter, who live this mission daily, has differentiated them in ways that make them almost impossible to copy.

Patagonia are an example of how organisations operating with good products, but that are not significantly different to competitors, can get a commercial advantage through attracting and retaining the best people. They were innovative and adaptable and listened to their people so that they created a working environment that attracted and retained the best people. By doing so, they gain an advantage in the marketplace without having to invent new technology.

Creating the right culture of people, recruiting the right people, and retaining the right people are clear advantages for businesses. As Patagonia demonstrated, by leveraging talented people, businesses can gain an advantage.

But it is essential that when you have talented people, you allow them to deliver. Leadership intransigence can damage results and illustrates the importance of succeeding with difficult people.

RESULTS COME FROM PEOPLE POWER

In 2005, Research In Motion, the company behind the ground-breaking BlackBerry phone, had a more than 50% smartphone market share.

Their CEO, Mike Lazaridis, had a clear strategy that led to their dominance and had assembled an excellent team of engineers who had developed a series of highly successful devices.

They focused on the enterprise market, using a combination of secure email and devices with an inbuilt keyboard to secure contracts with large corporations and governments.

They became synonymous with smartphones, and in the early 2000s, seats were filled with executives working intently on their Blackberrys when sitting on a train or waiting at an airport.

When I joined Roche as a Brand Manager in the UK, I was given my first Blackberry and was over the moon.

Features such as Blackberry Messenger, a secure instant message chat available years before WhatsApp was widely used, became staple tools for communicating with colleagues.

I sat on an underground train in London one day with my boss, who was able to work through dozens of emails while we travelled back from an agency meeting.

It was revolutionary and enabled millions to work on the move for the first time.

However, the talented engineering team at BlackBerry were not allowed to adapt to the changing market.

What they needed to deliver changed dramatically in 2007 when Apple launched the iPhone.

This new device offered more than email communications. It was an all-in-one revolution, containing your entire music library, email, web browser, and something innovative: mobile applications.

It triggered a market change towards consumer-led devices, spearheaded by Apple and Google via their iOS and Android operating systems. The old world of keyboards and secure email was insufficient, yet Mike Lazaridis did not allow the people in the business to change. He remained fixated on the old ways, and as the world moved on, BlackBerry became ever more irrelevant.

An incredible team that is not empowered and inspired to work towards the right objectives and tasks will fail.

BlackBerry phones lost significant market share, and by 2012, the CEO was forced to step down and admit that the company had made important mistakes.

Great companies that harness trust and empower great people can achieve wonderful things. Great people bring innovation, they overcome obstacles, and they evolve.

It is difficult people who hold back innovation, who create silos, who damage trust and stall performance. This book is all about how to understand and overcome difficult people and release the restraints to excellence.

Research in Motion delivered incredible performance with Black-Berry, a combination of great people and great products gave them a huge advantage in the marketplace.

But when the product was surpassed by better, more consumer-led products, and their people were not allowed to change to keep up, they quickly lost ground.

BlackBerrys were not good enough, and without the trust to create the next-generation product, they could not keep up. This is in contrast to Patagonia, where people were the heart of the difference, and the company set about building a culture to retain, develop, and leverage its strengths.

I spent 17 years in the pharmaceutical industry in sales, marketing and commercial roles.

These businesses are filled with talented people who all share powerful missions to transform healthcare for patients in need.

It is rare to find an industry that has such motivating organisational missions. Regardless of what is thought about the industry, one which remains deeply mistrusted around the world for good reason, the stated purpose of the companies is easy to align with.

At the centre of all the cultural directions is a stated focus on the needs of patients and the desire to cure disease, save lives and alleviate suffering.

What is also clear is that all this must be delivered while serving the demands of shareholders for profits.

These businesses are highly profitable, and the conflict between the desire to help people in need and the demand to maximise profits is the source of much debate and mistrust.

But my experience working in local operating companies demonstrated to me that they are not obsessed with profits, margins, and money—quite the opposite.

The focus on people and relationships was central within the teams that I worked with.

Businesses were willing and able to invest in people's development and supported talent from all backgrounds.

They also placed customer relationships at the centre of decision-making.

There are few purchasers of healthcare.

Governments or large insurance companies usually buy medicines and other products for their populations.

This dynamic leaves pharmaceutical companies in local markets with a limited number of people to work with, and these limited customers retain significant buying power.

The result was a perception that a strong relationship with these powerful buyers was essential for the business's survival, and this belief drove an obsession with being liked at the expense of delivering value.

I witnessed hundreds of meetings as an employee and dozens more as an external adviser, during which the fear of damaging a customer's relationship was so intense that it became the most critical factor in the decision.

On many occasions, organisations became so paralysed by fear that they made decisions that cost them significant amounts of money to avoid conflict.

A focus on retaining relationships within the organisation or with customers at the expense of a focus on delivering commercial results is expensive.

Businesses need to deliver results, or they will fail. When they fail, people lose their jobs, leaving customers disappointed.

The irony is that obsessing over the need to be liked destroys the relationships that were the centre of the decision-making.

In the same way that when a partner in a relationship who is afraid of being abandoned obsesses over where their significant other is, they ultimately drive them away, so it can be with businesses and people who are obsessed with being liked by customers and colleagues.

For businesses to succeed, they must balance results and relationships.

Great teams and talented people need a clear direction and operate with goals and boundaries that create an excellent culture that understands the importance of people and relationships and knows when it is time to focus on what is being delivered.

RESULTS & RELATIONSHIPS

I have been fortunate throughout my career to witness firsthand the culture of many different organisations.

Throughout my career, I have worked as an employee for five companies, and within those, I worked in different business units and locations.

As a client advisor, I have seen many companies either working on long-term projects, in interim roles or delivering events and programmes with snapshots.

Through my sporting career, I have also witnessed firsthand the culture of performance at various levels. I worked with some very talented coaches and players as a professional, but I also saw a variety of approaches at various representative levels.

Each gave me insight and experience into how leaders, managers, coaches and colleagues focused on the key priorities of results and relationships.

Their relative success in finding this potent balance indicates the group's success.

When I was 16, I was selected to play for the South Lancashire Rugby League team in a series of matches against Cumbria and North Lancashire.

The selection process involved selecting players from their respective town teams to attend a trial day. The trial day consisted of a series of 20-minute matches with a mixture of players, and in the end, selectors chose a squad.

I became familiar with this format during those years. It was used several times to choose representative teams in Rugby League and Rugby Union.

I hated it.

For players like me, it provided limited opportunities to demonstrate our skills because we relied on others to distribute the ball and operate as a team.

The format meant that, because of the system's nature, there was little incentive to include others in the team in the performance.

The same was true at the next stage.

Our matches against Cumbria and North Lancashire were used in the selection process to select a team representing North West Counties in a series against Yorkshire and ultimately build up to the full England squad.

This was a system built on results only.

Your progress through the system was measured by your ability to stand out and be noticed at the expense of your teammates.

During my time in that system, it was almost impossible for players to break out of their cliques.

Players came from small towns with close connections to other players. These friendships endured as friends were selected through the system, but given the selection process and the fact that on each weekend, these teammates would face off in local rivalries playing for their home town teams, there was little or no incentive to build trust with others.

This problem has haunted coaches and managers of representative teams for generations.

The capacity to break silos and build team unity is hard when rivalries are intense at the club level and time at the representative level is limited.

Those able to foster a strong team ethos have a significant advantage.

Rugby teams like the legendary New Zealand All Blacks, the current dominant Rugby World Cup Champions, the South African Springboks, and the Australian cricket team all implement a central contract system that enables the national team to better manage the time and commitments of key players and provide a clear set of priorities.

A central contract is one where the national body employs the players directly rather than the players being contracted to separate clubs.

This system gives the national body the authority to stop players from playing for the club, insist they are available for the national team and gather them for training when required.

It completely avoids the conflicts that exist when players are contracted to clubs and need permission to play for the national team.

In these cases, central contracts establish a clear expectation and understanding among the players that the national team should be their focus.

This clarity helps solve the problems of divided loyalties and drives the individuals together.

Excellent performance requires great people, but it also demands that these individuals unite, build trust, and collaborate.

But this is only half the story of finding a balance of results and relationships that deliver excellence.

Great people who feel a strong loyalty are useless if that loyalty and motivation aren't channelled in the right direction.

Working for Sanofi was a founding part of my commercial career and a critical part of my development. I progressed through several roles, starting as a sales representative and including marketing and management positions.

When I joined the company in the summer of 1999, I joined Lorex, which was about to be purchased by Sanofi to become Sanofi Synthelabo.

The product range was an exciting combination of new and innovative medicines, established and well-known brands and some historio but high-performing products.

But what struck me most, reflecting on my time in the business, was the focus on performance.

The UK managing director was a larger-than-life character who was well-known across the industry. Charismatic and charming, he was at ease amongst the commercial teams and would easily chat with everyone during events and meetings.

He created a culture of people bonded through connections forged through hard work, focus, ambition, and fun.

He was highly competitive and, on stage, would tell stories of his conversations with other Managing Directors during industry events.

He loved to discuss the looks on the faces of the leaders of competitor companies when he shared our latest growth figures.

Sanofi Synthelabo took enormous pride in being the underdog.

We were a medium-sized company, ranked only in the top 15 companies in the UK in terms of sales revenue, but we were growing fast.

We were united behind one goal: to enter the top five companies in the UK, and we were passionate about achieving it.

We met as a company 3 times per year to be briefed on the strategies for the next quarter.

There was a relentless focus on sales excellence. We constantly practised our sales meetings with each other. Our marketing teams were challenged to refresh and reinvigorate campaigns. We were given clear goals that could be broken down by day and set at industry-leading standards.

Everything was dedicated to making the sales team the most effective in the industry because that would drive growth.

Each meeting included a review of the recent numbers, and as a young man, I became conversant in the broader industry figures, data on growth, and sales value.

We would wait for the final presentation when the MD would give us the address, the latest numbers, and his compatriots' reactions.

We would leave inspired, motivated and determined.

We were the fastest-growing company in the UK between 1999 and 2005, climbing from number 18 to number 8 in sales against all odds.

The pinnacle moment was when the business's value was seen as so great that Sanofi Synthelabo acquired Aventis, a company larger in sales revenue then, and created one of the industry's biggest companies.

The UK team consisted of highly talented individuals, and during those years, we created enduring friendships and trusted one another's capabilities. Still, we were also united by a relentless and unforgiving dedication to achieving our business goals.

FLEXIBILITY, ADAPTATION & MAINTAINING A BALANCE

I have spent the last 30 years fascinated by high performers in sports and business.

I have read books, talked to experts, used my experiences and observations, and considered the essential elements carefully.

Performance is sustained when there is a balance between results and relationships.

People and businesses maintaining this balance have the best of both worlds.

They have an incredible culture of individuals who trust each other, communicate well, and build partnerships. But they can only deliver the results they do when the people in the culture are able to adapt to the people around them.

They never compromise on results and relationships as critical, but they can be flexible on their relative weighting in order to retain a strong culture.

They can extend this focus on trust to customers, building strong relationships that endure difficult moments, and they are seen as long-term partners.

Organisations that lose the balance and are unable to demonstrate flexibility to adapt when the situation demands it will struggle.

I used to work in a business for which results were all that mattered. We are pushed to constantly compete with others, similar to the selection process for representative teams.

Relationships, teamwork, and customer partnerships were secondary to results. Customers were simply a means to an end: to deliver revenue and profit goals.

The company did not prioritise important customer partnerships by offering a more relationship-focused approach; instead, they were relentless in chasing revenue.

There was no balance and no flexibility, and it damaged long-term success.

Jack Welch, CEO of GE, made the 'rank and yank' strategy famous and grew across other huge US and European businesses.

The plan is to rank all employees into one of three groups—the top 20%, the middle 70%, and the bottom 10%—and then sack the worst performers who appeared to be successful in the short term.

Organisations such as Ford, Conoco, Sun Microsystems, Cisco Systems, and Enron used the same approach, believing it removed underperformers and benefited the business and employees.

However, it was fiercely criticised for creating a toxic work culture in which employees were discouraged from collaborating and only interested in their performance.

Indeed, Enron became famous for the world's largest accounting scandal, which it can be argued was connected to this approach to place performance as the major driver of decisions leading to massive fraud and, ultimately, bankruptcy.

General Electric also struggled to retain its status as the world's largest company; today, it exists only as a brand name and not as a functioning business.

Ford and others abandoned the strategy because they were concerned about its effectiveness and faced legal challenges from employees who were unhappy with the subjective models used to assess performance, which could result in job loss.

The strategy to prioritise performance and results at the expense of everything else damages trust with employees, damages working relationships across the business and destroys partnerships with customers who can feel exploited by what could appear to be a selfish attitude to business.

However, an overreliance on relationships can be equally as costly to businesses without the headlines of bankruptcy and loss.

The impact of a culture where relationships take priority is less dramatic; instead, it demonstrates a slow decline in performance and stagnation.

A notable example of an over-dependence on customer relationships is the journey of MySpace.

MySpace dominated the internet and social media space before Facebook established itself. They allowed users to post online, share stories and blog posts and connect with others.

They built a strong following and grew fast as the popularity of the internet exploded.

However, with the emergence of Facebook, MySpace was slow to adapt. The user experience stagnated, becoming cluttered and difficult. Facebook's news feed feature offered something MySpace did not and attracted people in droves.

The challenge that MySpace faced was how to adapt. Did they choose to move away from their loyal and significant customer base, potentially upsetting them in the process, to become more like Facebook, or do they double down on their strategy and hold their ground, hoping to offer something different but appealing?

They chose to stick to their strategy, but even with that, they failed to evolve and deliver the clean, engaging interface that users were growing to expect.

A series of decisions, including technical choices, interface structure, strategy, and advertising revenue, left the MySpace site well behind Facebook's offering, and the company lost ground and unravelled.

This dilemma of upsetting existing customers and shifting to a new approach is common as businesses and products evolve.

It taps into our fear of loss and rejection and is a primal protection strategy that protects us from risks.

How businesses deal with this dilemma says a lot about their preference for results and relationships, and whether they have the right balance.

They faced such a dilemma while I worked at GSK in the 2010s.

One of their most significant and successful products was replaced by a newer product, including improved devices designed to improve patient experience and new medicines that demonstrated enhanced effectiveness.

The company was excited about the launch, and CEO Andrew Whitty invested heavily in new manufacturing facilities and other infrastructure to make the new launches successful.

But they had a problem.

The existing product was still incredibly popular, and sales continued to increase. The treatment was well-liked by patients and doctors and contributed significantly to the revenue of the GSK business.

How were the teams supposed to communicate about the new product?

The new product was starting from zero. It had no sales and no long-term reputation over the previous decade, and although the business believed it to be a significant progression in treatment, there were sceptics.

If asked, "Should we stop using the previous treatment and start with this one?" The answer was clear: yes. The new product would benefit newly identified people.

However, when asked, "Should we switch patients from the current treatment to the new treatment?" the response was unclear.

The risk of supporting a widespread switch was patients would be unhappy about the change and perhaps move to a competitor's product, costing sales and risking the reputation of the new product.

My experience working in various business units across GSK was a business where relationships mattered.

Groups of leaders made decisions, discussed ideas, and reached a consensus. To be inclusive, voices were heard, and great lengths were gone to in order to be inclusive.

The business cared about customers' thoughts and focused on patients' experiences.

It was a place of work where many people worked very hard to ensure that the interests of others were at the heart of the business.

But it was also a place where decisions were debated and revisited. Time was wasted gathering information because if it was suggested that more information was needed, the culture found it hard to reject that and make a decision.

Meetings often overran because a highly inclusive culture seemed to find it hard to restrict agenda topics, close down discussions and force timing.

I witnessed several corporate attempts to make meetings more productive and sharpen their execution.

In my opinion, it was an experience of a company that tilted too far towards the need to be liked and to focus on the relationship at the cost of results.

Contrast their dilemma when launching a new product with the actions of Apple when a new iPhone is launched, and it is easy to see the difference.

When a new version of the iPhone is launched, it builds on billions of dollars of revenue and highly advanced technology. Each new version is heralded with fanfare about its technological advances.

When a new version replaces an older one, the same fanfare is heard, and there is no debate from Apple. They stop selling the old version, and the new one becomes the king. They encourage the trade-in of older versions and back the latest phone to be as successful as the last.

Replacing a mobile phone is not the same as switching patients from one medication to another when they are stable and doing well. GSK could not or should not have stopped selling the older product. Still, a clear vision that the new product is an advance and that there is a single-minded approach to its success would have looked very different in how it was discussed inside the business and with customers.

A balance of results and relationships means the courage to make decisions that people may not like. Businesses exist to make money. They create needed products and services and sell them profitably to customers.

This fundamental truth should guide businesses and their employees. Decisions should be made that help improve business performance.

The business needs a clear set of targets and goals, and people must be accountable for delivery. Rewards and incentives should be provided to reward excellence.

However, to sustain long-term performance, the business must maintain strong relationships with customers, suppliers, employees, and stakeholders.

Employees must be encouraged to collaborate, learn, and embrace change to create a positive culture. They should also understand the importance of strong partnerships with customers and suppliers that endure as long as they deliver results.

A clear set of values that guide behaviour, a business mission anchored in contributing positively to the community and the world, and strategies that promote long-term value all support a focus on relationships.

Businesses need a culture that balances results and relationships to survive and thrive. The people within that organisation also need that balance because their actions drive the culture.

No two people are the same regarding their beliefs and attitudes. We are each a product of our genetics, our environment, and the business cultures we work within.

Within the most successful and unsuccessful businesses, there is a mixture of people, each with their own interpretation of the importance of results and relationships.

Both these elements drive us all, and how we prioritise them sets the tone for our work and collaboration.

During my corporate career, I worked in many different businesses, each with a similar business model: selling medicines that improve the health and well-being of people in need. However, each had a very different culture, and I felt more or less at home with each, depending on the culture I encountered.

When we encounter difficult people at work, we usually meet someone who sees the balance between results and relationships differently.

When I deliver a training event to clients, I explain the balance model. I remember running a programme for a group at the famous racecourse in Epsom.

On the first afternoon, I stood in front of the group and explained the model, emphasising the shortcomings of the imbalance. One participant smiled when I discussed an overemphasis on relationships, causing meetings to overrun. I stopped and looked at her for a moment. I asked her, "Does this resonate?" She nodded and laughed. " That's me!" she said, "All my meetings overrun, and I am obsessed with being liked!"

Her focus on that programme became immediately apparent and shifted back towards delivering results for her team.

She struggled to deal with people who wanted to get down to business and who wanted to optimise terms. Her emphasis on relationships not only meant that meetings often ran over with people she liked, but also that she gave away price to those who challenged her directly, because she was so afraid of creating upset that she believed it was the best way to be liked.

She found dealing with people stressful, and she was aware of the pressure from her manager and colleagues to deliver more.

Her preferences and instincts created tension with her customers and her colleagues.

She did not intend to be difficult; in fact, the opposite. But people with different perceptions of the balance found her so.

And so it is with difficult people. As we will explore in this book, nobody sets out to be difficult. They have positive intentions, yet conflict results from poor communication, misunderstandings, and differences in values.

They might feel that results are more important to them than relationships. If we believe that relationships are the priority, then we have a problem. It is nobody's fault, but it will cause tension between us.

In this case, the other person is likely to judge you as the difficult one, because naturally, we choose to blame others!

The harsh truth is that there is a problem between you and you, or they, might be at fault.

You blame them, they blame you - but someone needs to act to improve the situation.

The ability to adapt, accommodate and be flexibile is the art of getting the elephant out of the room. If everyone has a different perception of balance and problems arise when the differences create tension, then the solution is to adapt.

That will become your superpower.

In the following sections, I will describe various types of difficult people at work, so that you can understand their motives and emotions.

This insight will give you the opportunity to change your approach to be more easily understood and to better influence their behaviours.

Consider the people whom you find difficult; where do they fit? But consider yourself, too.

Recognising your style as a colleague, manager, and customer will provide you with powerful insight into where areas of problems might exist and what you can do to change them.

In this book, we will explore trust, difficult conversations, and seeing the world through their eyes.

I will share some checklist tools for you to use to prepare for discussions, but most of all, this book is a chance for you to reflect on problems, take responsibility for them and figure out what is needed to change things.

Getting the elephant out of the room requires accountability, control of emotions, listening, and change.

In this section, we have seen how much people, relationships and performance are connected for businesses.

We need people to deliver excellence, and therefore we seek a balance of results and relationships; where there are differences in belief of the status of the balance, that is where we discover difficult people and where we must learn to adapt in order to succeed.

Perception is everything, which is why understanding how others see the world sits at the centre.

Where do you see things differently from colleagues, managers and customers? Once you understand this, you will begin to grasp how to rebalance and resolve issues.

SECTION 02:
DIFFICULT COLLEAGUES

SILOED WORKING

In 2004, I moved across the UK to take on a position as a regional sales manager, leading a team of 12 people across four territories just North of London.

It was a territory in a beautiful part of the UK famous for its universities, coastline, country estates, and houses occupied by the gentry of England and movie stars such as Brad Pitt and Angelina Jolie, who owned a home there.

The major centres were Oxford, Cambridge, Norwich and Reading. The region covered a semi-circle that followed the path of the M25 north of London and was bordered by the Norfolk and Suffolk coastline on one side and the M4 connecting London to Wales on the other.

I chose to live in Northampton, which was situated right in the middle of the four territories and gave me access to all of them via major east/west roads.

The team I joined in the region was a fascinating mix of people.

There were some people with decades of experience in the industry and the company, plus some newcomers.

They were also a team that presented a different culture to the rest of the business unit. An academic group, they were thoughtful and reflective. They discussed and debated technical details and science, and appreciated good food, great conversation, and calm.

The rest of the business was built on teams of youthful exuberance, a culture of a can-do attitude, courage, and acting before thinking. It was a competitive business working in a tough market, and it generally reflected people who wanted to take on challenges and succeed.

When I joined the group, they had been without a manager for a while. As a result, they felt unloved and outside the norm.

While other teams had been celebrating with their managers at drinks receptions, this group were left sitting quietly on their own.

It generated a sense of mistrust of the rest of the business. This team saw itself as different. They were united in that difference, and it created a bond.

Equally, the rest of the business was suspicious of this group. They were different, and that created a space.

When I was appointed, I was invited to a conversation with the business unit head to learn more about the team I would lead.

He took pride in knowing everyone on the team of more than 100 people, but he was also quick to judge and determined to create a performance culture built on the framework of his design.

This group did not fit that design well.

He saw that as a challenge, and during our conversation in his glass office, he walked me through the team's personalities individually. He described their strengths and what they brought to the business, but mostly described his perception of the challenges they presented and where he saw the future.

He foresaw a change in the team and wanted me to understand where that change would come from. "This is a difficult team, with difficult people," he told me dryly.

I prepared myself for a tough time. This move to the centre of England would not be all countryside, rolling hills and sunshine.

This was my second opportunity to lead a team, and I had learned much in my previous role. This time, I felt confident and determined to bring my personality into the role.

Previously, I had listened too intently to others who wanted to tell me how to work. I followed their advice and made mistakes.

I realised that I was not them. Their communication style did not work for me. Conversations became clumsy because they ran against my instincts and were delivered unnaturally.

This time was different.

I spent time with my new team.

Because of how they had been managed, they felt abandoned, unloved, and distant from the business. Despite being close to London, their land felt at the other end of the world, not less than an hour from the head office.

I joined them daily, sharing the car with them and getting to know their ways of thinking and challenges. I grew to understand them, and we built trust.

I also saw the flaws.

This was a relationship team. They saw people as a priority, bonded over a shared sense of distance, and became close.

However, performance was poor. They failed to deliver against sales targets, and the fundamentals of sales excellence were missing.

They lacked enthusiasm. They were not spending enough time with customers and engaged in scientific and technical debates and discussions, which, whilst academically stimulating, did not progress the business.

In the business context, there was a classical group of difficult people.

They were different, measured themselves in ways inconsistent with the rest of the business, and operated differently.

It was easy to see why my boss wanted change. He was frustrated by underperformance, which was slowing the growth of the business unit and damaging his reputation.

My challenge was to deliver change but also to provide performance.

The question was how to bring this group back into the same way of thinking as the rest of the business without being seen as someone simply imposing rules that they objected to, without being frozen out of the group as they closed ranks.

My time invested in building trust and understanding them was a key foundation, as were some of the concessions I made to work how they wanted to work.

The typical sales team meeting for the rest of the business involved listening to presentations on company performance and then spending the evening drinking in a bar.

That was not what this team needed.

They also found themselves on a large geography where hours could be spent travelling to a venue, with those in the centre benefiting from central locations and those on the edges always being asked to travel.

I made changes. I wanted this mature and thoughtful group to take ownership and be accountable to each other. I wanted them to enjoy time together and focus on the right performance elements.

We began to share the hosting of sales meetings with each territory responsible for finding a venue, making arrangements and booking a lunch or dinner at a high-quality restaurant, something very important to them.

The content of the meetings changed, too. Events became involving and engaging. We would participate in business games and challenges designed to get us talking about our issues. We created shared learning experiences.

We created a personal identity that generated a sense of identity, underlining the bond and bringing us closer to the main business.

We took the business values and challenged ourselves to describe the behaviours relevant to our team that matched these values. We prioritised three of the values as a focal point for us, and we set them into a team charter with standards.

All the ownership came from the group. Their behaviours based on their priorities turned into a charter for performance.

This created a foundation for change that made life easy for me. The majority of the team was ambitious. They did not like the culture of the main business unit; they worked differently, but they wanted success and recognition.

This charter was the platform they needed to drive standards, create evidence to justify promotions and build confidence from a series of successes.

Except for one.

One person was struggling.

He was one of the team's older members. He had enjoyed a successful career spanning many years but struggled to keep up with the changing world.

He wanted to live in a world where customers were old friends, and visiting them was a social event.

Operating in a tough market with competitors and customers who demanded excellence was too much for him.

My boss had singled him out as someone he wanted to leave the team on my first day, but at that moment, it was impossible.

The rest of the group adored him.

The younger people looked to him for guidance, and his kindness and nurturing nature were highly valued.

Inoffensive, stable and experienced, he held the group together during their time in the wilderness.

The group considered the team without him unthinkable, but management, which needed results, considered a team with him impossible.

It had become clear that he was in a different place from the rest of us. Leadership judged him difficult and problematic, but I saw something else.

I saw a man who was not willing or able to change. He was not trying to be difficult, but that was the impression he gave when the business was changing so fast, and he was not.

One rainy afternoon, I sat in the car with him after another disappointing day, having seen no customers.

After nine months of working together, I still hadn't seen him meet customer expectations for visits, and the time had come to address this head-on.

We sat quietly, listening to the rain on the car's roof outside Peterborough Hospital, when I turned to him and set out my challenge.

I told him he would be on a performance improvement plan because I struggled to justify his performance and the standards needed to improve.

He looked at me with sad eyes, nodding in agreement.

We put the plan in place and began to monitor results.

A few weeks later, the whole business unit travelled to a company event at a hotel in London. The senior leadership addressed us and referenced the Apollo missions as inspiration for the next few years of growth, delivering the impossible.

On return, the Chief People Officer called me with some news. The team member approached him during the event and asked about early retirement. He had had enough and saw it was his time to leave.

He decided he was not right for the position and announced it to the team. A few weeks later, we went for dinner with the business unit head and a team of friends to celebrate a long and distinguished career.

With the right circumstances, we had changed a culture of isolation and protection, a group of difficult people, into one where they were happy to say goodbye to someone everyone knew was no longer right for the business.

Forming Silos

Sometimes, difficult colleagues are those who create their own culture within the culture of the business.

Have you ever had to find ways to work with particular departments and teams that seem to work in their own way, according to their own rules, and do not follow the rest of the business?

I had encountered that in my team. They were not deliberately creating their own culture, but they had evolved that way due to their age, experience, and lack of leadership.

It is different if you have people actively trying to create their cult. One example that springs to mind is IT.

In businesses, the IT team is often a bolt-on group that provides a very specific function to procure, manage, and monitor equipment that is now essential for normal working.

They rarely need to cooperate with other groups, so they can afford their idiosyncrasies. If this group works the way they like, assuming they are excellent at delivering the service and security needed, there is little risk to the business.

But what about other teams? Have you experienced groups that create their silos, and as a result, you find it challenging to work together and communicate easily?

Nokia had a long and illustrious history before losing its place as the global leader in mobile phone technology when Microsoft bought it in 2014.

It was founded in 1865 as a paper mill in Finland. It expanded into other technologies and was consistently at the forefront of mobile phone technology evolution.

They were the first to launch a car phone in 1982 and perform GSM phone calls in 1991. By the early 2000s, they had dominated the mobile phone market, with a 50% market share, for almost a decade.

Their devices were renowned for being user-friendly and durable; the Nokia 1100 and 1110 were best sellers.

I remember walking into a mobile shop in the early 2000s and upgrading my handset to the latest Nokia, which had interchangeable cases and was small enough to fit in my pocket.

I was an early adopter and took great pride in my cutting-edge phone.

Nokia was a leader in more than phones. They were instrumental in network development and setting industry standards, and they were well aware that, as leaders, they had the power to shape the whole industry.

However, things went very wrong for Nokia in the early 2000s with the launch of smartphones and BlackBerry.

The question is how?

How could the global leader in technology, with a dominant market share and footholds in the networks that ran the whole system, suddenly and dramatically be left behind by competitors?

Part of the answer can be found in the way that Nokia operated.

Within the business existed silos and groups working independently. They made decisions independently and with little cohesion. There was no clear overall strategy for the industry, meaning that it was hard for them to react cohesively and quickly when they were surprised by disruptive technology and companies that previously were not competitors.

Until the early 2000s, their major competitors were companies like Motorola, which made similar devices. They had never had to compete with businesses like Apple, Samsung, and RIM.

Some teams focused on developing advanced technologies; others worked on existing devices and protected current sales. These departments competed for internal resources, creating tension that slowed change.

Within a few years, their market share fell from over 40% to less than 5%, and Microsoft stepped in to buy them. Microsoft also had challenges at the time. They had missed out on the mobile market and saw Nokia as a way into the phone sector, which was quickly leaving them behind.

How do these silos form?

Empire Building

There are very few people at the top of any organisation. There is only one Chief Executive Officer, one Chief Finance Officer, and one Chief Marketing Officer, yet tens of thousands of people can work in the business.

That means there is little space for ambitious people to rise through the ranks to seniority. Without a real development prospect, people become frustrated, disenfranchised, and rebellious.

The aspiring leaders who cannot win status are likely to challenge those with the power and authority to try and dethrone them, causing a huge risk to the few powerful leaders.

It is a much better strategy to provide opportunities for others in the business to make progress, be given authority, and be awarded status.

They focus on personal development and feel rewarded for the position they earn. They also become advocates and supporters of the leaders who gave them this opportunity.

Instead of dealing with competitors, the executives have advocates.

This approach flows through organisations, establishing a series of pyramids with leaders at the top. These leaders aspire to rise through the next pyramid, and others below them aspire to rise through the one they are in.

This strategy also allows complex businesses to thrive. Decision-making and creativity can be spread through complex teams and across huge geographies. Well-organised businesses can, over time, spread worldwide, forming multiple divisions, complex functions, manufacturing, supply chains, and financial structures.

From within these functions and divisions, it can be hard to understand the level of complexity that exists around you, with parallel teams operating, with whom you might never meet.

I worked for companies such as GSK. At the time, they were a global organisation with huge brands sold in supermarkets, pharmacies, hospitals, vaccination clinics, cancer clinics and general practice. Research and development, manufacturing, finance, supply chains, and more supported the sales and commercial teams. Within the commercial functions I worked in, different divisions sold over-the-counter products and pharmaceuticals. There were different country structures and different organisations above country managing leadership and decision making.

When I walked into the bewildering global head office in London, where everyone worked, I was hardly even aware of these teams.

Thousands of people worked there across all these complex functions, and only a handful knew each other in any group.

We worked for the same business, but in totally different spheres.

These mini businesses are the only way to operate, but keeping them aligned, efficient and productive is a significant challenge.

Noticing the complexity of large global businesses helps us understand why Nokia found it so difficult to adapt quickly to competition and significant changes to customers' demands.

But this complexity creates space for difficult people to create their own world.

They can use their power and influence to shape a working environment as they want to, creating an 'us versus them' mentality that helps cement their position.

I have witnessed this at the country level, where country leadership argues that their markets are different from other markets and, therefore, need to be treated differently with their systems and processes, products, and unique marketing strategies.

I have also seen this within markets where a divisional head builds a culture separate from other divisions and even generates tension between colleagues working in the same physical geography, but on different brands

I remember working in this situation during my time at Sanofi. We had two blockbuster products, each sold by different divisions.

The leadership, especially the sales leadership, made no secret of their differences and built very different operating cultures.

The brands had different customer profiles, and the way to build success for them was different. However, this division went further.

It was like a competition. Which sales team was the best, most effective organisation?

Despite working in the same geographies with mirrored territories and covering very similar customer groups, the divisions had very limited connection and cooperation.

It was down to local management and local relationships to build bridges with no formal process to find synergies between colleagues facing the same challenges in the market.

The attraction of creating these differing cultures is obvious for the group's leaders.

By carving out a specific culture, they build a personal kingdom that they are in charge of. They can create a way of communicating, operating, and thinking that puts them in charge.

It is a tempting prospect for people who value status, like a shortcut to a more senior position. Instead of recognising the real place in the system, perhaps lower than dreamed, they create a space where they rule, separate from everything else.

Breaking Down Silos

We have discussed the importance of balancing results and relationships to develop and sustain high performance and a high-performance culture.

The challenge with a siloed mentality is that this balance may exist - within the walls of the silo. The question to reflect on is whether the behaviour is damaging wider business performance.

The existence of a culture within the culture could be a helpful addition if the organisation deliberately tries to cultivate alternative ways of working to deliver specific strategic goals, perhaps innovation.

However, it is likely to cause difficulties whenever the group comes into contact with the rest of the organisation, and the more frequently this happens and the more commonly these different cultures exist, the greater the internal tensions that will exist.

To address siloed working, the first issue to address is performance, followed by relationships.

A business is defined by what it delivers, and therefore, it is much easier to address performance problems because these are tangible and more straightforward to measure and track.

It is also easier to hold leaders of these siloes to account for inability to deliver results because of their more measurable elements.

But that is not the end of the story.

A bigger problem for a business in terms of siloes are teams who deliver results but do not fit to corporate ways of working.

Indeed, these teams could consider their non-adherence to corporate ways of working a key reason for their success.

Creating a counterculture within the business, a team of rebels who deliver results in their own way holds a particular attraction for people working in the group.

It is well established that creating a sense of otherness can be a powerful unifying mission, even within a business.

However, in time, this counterculture will become damaging because of the friction it causes in the rest of the business, and issues must be addressed.

There is a way to bring teams into the main fold by using the established business values and working methods. These values are set from the highest levels of the business and guide expected behaviours from everyone in the organisation.

In most organisations, the business has commercial goals to drive results supported by a vision statement.

They also have a mission statement supported by values, behaviours and ways of engaging with each other.

People often complain that these are simply signs on the wall and do not directly affect daily operations. Still, that is not the case for many businesses, especially when leaders use them to guide actions.

For groups operating as a culture within the culture, these values and behaviours provide a path back to the business.

A group that delivers results but does so by acting in ways inconsistent with these values, perhaps aspects such as collaboration and communication, can be held to account.

Behaviours provide a direct way to track what is said and done in certain circumstances. With the support of influential people, it is possible to use examples of actions that were inconsistent with business values and discuss alternatives.

The goal is not to stifle performance or kill creativity; it is to accelerate both for the good of the whole organisation.

As we saw with Nokia, high-performing groups that do not align create friction that can destroy business performance.

NEGATIVE, UNCOOPERATIVE, RESISTANT TO CHANGE

Spencer Silver was a chemist working for 3M in 1968. Like many of his colleagues, he worked on experiments to identify the next industrial adhesive. 3M had forged a name for creating industrial chemicals at the heart of technological advancement, and they were seeking ways to consolidate their position.

But Spencer Silver had discovered something different.

The adhesive he had identified was neither powerful nor strong nor quick drying. It was the opposite.

He had developed an adhesive that was sticky, but would not fix permanently; in fact, it remained sticky and could allow objects to be moved once fixed.

In addition, once moved, it left no sticky residue where it had been.

Spencer Silver was excited, and he took it to the business leadership, whom he anticipated could find ways to turn this creation into a significant company asset. His excitement quickly turned to dismay when the leadership rejected his invention.

They were seeking the next industrial adhesive, and this product was nothing like what they were looking for. His idea was rejected, and he was ignored.

He continued to pitch his idea for another 12 years without success until a use was finally identified, by accident.

Spencer's colleague had become frustrated at church because bookmarks were continually falling from his hymn book during the service, causing him to lose his place.

If only there was something he could use to stick a paper on the pages and mark his place without damaging the delicate paper of the book, he complained to Spencer one day.

"I have just the thing," Spencer replied, spreading a thin layer of his adhesive on the back of some papers before placing them on the appropriate pages.

It was a revelation, and the Post-It note was born. This invention was so significant that it transformed the stationary cupboards of almost every office on earth and catapulted 3M to become a household name.

Spencer Silver had discovered something wonderful and highly valuable to his company, but imagine if you, or one of your colleagues, had been an executive in the leadership at the time.

How would you have seen him?

Uncooperative, negative, resistant to change?

Was he a difficult person who frustrated those around him?

I hear regularly of the difficulties of dealing with negativity and resistance to change. It is said that colleagues reject new systems and processes, customers refuse to adopt new products, and staff members are set in their ways.

An entire industry is built around implementing change across organisations, and it only exists to deal with difficult people who refuse to change.

When organisations adopt new software systems, expensive investments are made to speed up production, make life easier and provide additional capabilities. After the sales teams leave, customer success teams arrive.

Customer success teams in the software and technology industry are there to support the adoption of new systems because of the negativity, uncooperativeness, and difficulty experienced by customers who have bought the system.

Products that are sold have built into the costs of purchase the fees required to support a team of people who exist to help customers with uncooperative people who, for many reasons, do not use services.

Organisations made changes due to changes in market conditions, evolutions in product design, new technologies and of course to find efficiencies and cost savings.

However, research shows that most of these changes fail for one reason or another.

Why is this all the case?

Are managers all surrounded by people who are difficult, uncooperative and negative?

Are they sitting at workstations, in offices and on shop floors simply refusing to use new software, to adopt new ways of working and simply rejecting change.

Sometimes, yes.

That could be precisely what is happening.

I worked with some representatives in the rail industry in the UK. Everyone agrees that this industry desperately needs change. Yet, rail companies and trade unions cannot agree on what change should happen and how it should be delivered.

Part of this is because trade unions do not accept the industry's current structure and refuse to cooperate to make it function. They want fundamental change to be delivered.

From the management perspective, they deal with groups of people who reject change, refuse to adapt to new ways of working, and are uncooperative.

However, from the trade unions' point of view, the world is very different.

They want to embrace more change than is being proposed. They want a fundamental reorganisation of the system.

It can be argued that what they want is backwards-looking and irrelevant, but they advocate change.

It is not change that they object to, just the type of change.

This reaction is typical of so-called uncooperative and difficult people.

I have spoken with consultants who specialise in implementing change across organisations, and a constant message they share is that when they explore the details, there are reasons why staff are resistant to the changes implemented by leaders. However, these same people are not especially resistant to changes they think will be valuable; they just believe that the valuable changes are not implemented.

Think about the people you know who are negative, uncooperative, and resistant to change. What impact do they have on you and others?

They become like rocks in the middle of flowing water.

Business goes around them, and people continue to make calls, think of new ideas, and engage with each other and customers. Most of all, they work together with the hope of success.

These rocks prevent business from flowing well and easily. The water is forced to divert around them, finding new ways to progress but getting slower.

Over time, the weight and pressure of the water can have an erosive effect, grinding down the stones into smaller stones that are less of a problem. However, this takes time and energy that many businesses cannot afford.

When these rocks pile up, stack together, and even coordinate, they become a wall that stops the flow altogether, and this is the fear held by leaders and colleagues who are determined to do the right thing.

As organisations evolve, we must all adapt, learn, and grow; otherwise, we become like these people—blockers.

Let's explore some of these blockers' behaviours for a moment to better understand their tactics and how they make our lives so difficult.

Do you know the person in the meetings who always finds a problem with the new idea?

Do you know the person for whom the meeting leader announces that all ideas are welcome and we will filter them later, because they anticipate that person who will automatically reject ideas?

Business is full of wicked questions. A wicked question is one without right or wrong; it is just a matter of opinion. Negative, uncooperative, and resistant people always seem to argue from a different perspective than the majority.

When the team discusses changes that should solve certain problems, these people find an issue with the new way or want to stick to the current method.

They can use a variety of tactics to be difficult.

- Find problems with the ideas that are being suggested
- Ask questions about details that are not yet considered, and reject the whole plan because they do not get an answer
- Ask for evidence that changes will make a tangible difference and reject any data as insignificant.
- Argue that there are no problems with the current way
- Suggest that smaller changes to current approaches are sufficient.
- Come up with new ideas that appear different from the current direction.
- Refuse to listen

They might be the people who want to constantly drive changes in the current ways of working.

I have lost count of the times I have heard a colleague use the phrase 'not fit for purpose'.

It is a common statement to be uncooperative when implementing ideas or changes. Difficult people describing a current or new way of working as not fit for purpose create significant challenges for businesses.

I am curious about the voices within organisations worldwide as new artificial intelligence (AI) tools are being more commonly used and integrated into processes.

Undoubtedly, there will be challenges and problems with systems unable to deliver exactly as planned immediately. This is precisely when people who are uncooperative, negative and resistant to change will be heard.

Are They Really That Difficult?

This book describes difficult people and their behaviours and ideas, but it is mostly about how to succeed despite them.

To succeed, we need to understand them. What is going on from their point of view?

Was Spencer Silver, the creator of Post-It Notes from 3M, whom I referred to at the start of the chapter, really being difficult?

He had invented something that turned out to be a huge commercial success for the business, and it was rejected because it did not fit within the current portfolio.

His difficult behaviour turned out to be persistence, and this persistence ensured that 3M launched a considerable success.

Your colleagues rejecting ideas, arguing for different ideas, asking questions about details, and challenging systems that are not fit for purpose are doing so for what they believe to be perfectly rational and logical reasons.

There will also be illogical reasons driving their actions.

These are likely to be political, emotional, and self-serving, which can make them harder to empathise with, but in reality, they are the major driving force behind them.

Difficult people, who resist change, are uncooperative, and are negative, are likely to think that they are helping you identify problems that need to be solved.

They will highlight the problems with your ideas, ask for details, and reject changes until they are ironed out because they want to ensure that everything runs smoothly and is seamless later.

Have they experienced ill-considered change before? Did they have to work through the consequences of problems that were not spotted, and as such, do they feel it is a duty to spare others this pain by pointing out issues?

When Terminal 5 at Heathrow Airport opened in March 2008, there were enormous baggage problems. This meant that thousands of bags were not loaded onto aircraft, and travellers were left at destinations worldwide with no luggage.

Technology problems needed to be resolved, and passengers' compensation claims were huge and costly. Plus, reuniting passengers with their lost luggage was a challenge.

It was a huge logistical, technological and financial disaster for the airport and airlines.

Imagine if you had been involved in sorting out that mess. I am sure you would have taken extra care to ensure that future projects were fully considered and tested to avoid the same issues.

The difficult people asking difficult questions do their best to ensure that new ideas are properly considered.

One of the additional complexities is the differing levels of detail that we each need to feel satisfied.

Perhaps there are differences between you and these people about how much detail they need to feel satisfied?

Someone needing more will question, reject and challenge proposals they consider ill thought through.

I observe that changes proposed by managers are often not fully considered before they are announced, tempting those who need details to reject them.

Leaders know they must involve teams in implementation or have legal responsibilities to talk to colleagues, so they announce headlines without details.

Difficult people can take this as rushed thinking and create barriers to change.

The emotional side of their behaviour is more complex and challenging. While the details of a plan can be worked out, problems identified, and contingencies considered, emotional barriers that portray themselves as uncooperative, rejecting, and challenging can be harder to unravel.

There could be a belief that these people are important, and their ego feels bruised by ideas that are not theirs, ideas that challenge their position through new methods that reduce their significance in the team or that they have not been involved enough in decisions.

The launch of AI tools in the coming years will likely generate a new flood of these feelings.

People in roles previously untouched by the spread of automation could now find their ways of working significantly altered and their roles diminished, as they see them.

One of my uncles was a print setter - a very artistic person employed by newspapers and magazines to design the layout of the pages, where photos were located, their size, the space for text and so on.

When digitisation and computers became widespread in publishing during the 1980s, he lost his job. Unwilling or unable to change, he never worked again.

This fear of loss could be significant in the hearts of people resistant to change.

A fear of losing status and losing their security through the risk of redundancy could be central to rejection.

There could also be a loss of control due to driving negativity. It can be a very challenging emotional state when we feel disempowered and feel that others are in control of our decisions.

It is somehow connected to childhood, when we have no power to live our lives. Consider the teenage years, when we transition from child to adult. These feelings are especially frustrating because we can make choices, but are not allowed.

If these feelings arise during change, then it is understandable that people resist, because they need to feel part of the decision and not disempowered bystanders.

We are not only driven by fears; there are also drivers of motivation that could play a role in these behaviours.

Spencer Silver was not fearful of losing anything. He was trying to gain recognition.

Far from being a rock in the stream of 3M, trying to slow down the organisation, he sought to divert some of the flow into a new direction that could even be faster than the current path.

He was not a barrier to change, but an opportunity to see additional value.

It just takes the right level of understanding to see the difference.

The resistant person may have ideas that they believe will deliver results and want recognition.

We are driven by a need to be seen as clever, and therefore creating ideas, or even finding problems in current ideas that nobody else has spotted, provides a source for this recognition.

Far from being difficult, there are emotions at the heart of this person that are positive and hopeful, but are selfish.

Overcoming Negativity

There is excellent evidence that implementing change by using force does not work.

An organisation can't implement change simply by announcing and forcing changes on the business.

There is a huge industry surrounding change management, and as a result, it is a well-researched topic.

The processes are not only used to deal with negativity, but to accelerate change and to ensure that views and options are fully considered.

Consensus suggests that there are five stages to the implementation of change.

These are leadership commitment, clear communication, employee involvement, structured change management and strategic planning.

They are all connected, and through them, they each contribute to overcoming difficult, negative, uncooperative and resistant people.

Suppose the motivation behind difficulties is to be seen as important, valuable and smart. If the personal drivers need to see problems others cannot see and get credit for them, employee engagement is a perfect tool to reduce the difficulties.

During employee involvement, colleagues will have many opportunities to have their ideas heard, suggest different ways to solve problems, and identify potential risk areas.

With the proper oversight and involvement of senior people, it is easy to notice these contributions and to recognise the people for them.

It creates an opportunity for colleagues to feel empowered during a change process.

Colleagues' involvement during change design and development can address barriers such as disempowerment, a lack of feeling valued, the need to be seen as intelligent, and fear of ill-considered implementation.

Fears of loss of status and security are harder to manage if the changes lead to significant changes in roles. Still, they too can be minimised through proper communication.

Change is usually motivated by necessity. Pressure to adapt to a changing world, the advance of technology, or emerging competition creates risk for the future.

A refusal to adapt can create a feeling of safety in the short term, but it also leads to the need for greater change in the long term, with often more dramatic consequences.

Properly considered and communicated change will likely be a programme of evolution over time, designed to slowly move the business towards the future.

Change is constant, and when it is directly connected to a consistently communicated business strategy and mission, there is often less difficulty.

Indeed, I interviewed David Ford, an experienced Human Resources leader from the Life Sciences Industry, on this topic, and he was clear that this approach is exactly how businesses can deliver change to teams fearful of the impact of change on them.

He explained that it is less of a surprise, it connects to a vision that they are aware of and is part of what could be considered business as usual.

I notice that great performance cultures can accept change as part of their way of operating because everyone accepts the need to adapt.

That manifests itself in the need to continue personal development of skills and knowledge, the need to evolve systems and processes, and the need to constantly recruit talent to replace those who can no longer deliver the group's standards.

When this is accepted, there is less resistance to change.

Summary

Uncooperative, resistant and rejecting people are not necessarily trying to be difficult.

They could be operating from a positive intention.

This creates challenges because I know of many companies with phrases like 'positive intent' embedded in their values. These companies struggle with difficult people who reject ideas and are uncooperative. There is a sense that these people are not operating in line with the company values, but that might not be true.

These people could be trying to ensure that mistakes are not made, that good ideas are not overlooked, that details are considered fully, and that they are given credit for their efforts.

Some others are fearful, but perhaps this too is justified.

They might fear losing the status they have worked hard to achieve, their jobs entirely, or losing control of their lives.

Understanding these beliefs and feelings gives us enough insight to address them and reduce the risk that these people become huge blockers in our teams.

Not everything requires a huge change management programme, but the approach's principles provide steps that we can use to resolve difficulties.

I argue that using change management as a process could often cause problems because it demonstrates a culture that is not constantly evolving.

Do you invest enough time paying attention to the team, listening to ideas and taking on good ones?

When I took over the team I talked about in the previous chapter, I was keen that they were all part of the journey of evolution and had the space to contribute.

I also think the gentleman who left the team did so because he saw the need to constantly evolve. He decided he would rather make other changes and leave the business. He took ownership of that decision to change, and as such, there was no resentment from him or the rest of his close colleagues.

Take time to advocate for change and be positive about its benefits.

Have open conversations with your colleagues about the changes and listen to their concerns and questions. Other points of view are always valuable because they help us see things we might not have spotted alone.

Involve people around you in the design, development, and implementation of ideas. This takes time, increases complexity, and can feel slow and cumbersome. However, when people are involved, they feel better. Critically, you generate better, more considered solutions and reduce negativity and barriers.

You seek to understand the emotional barriers to uncooperative behaviours and address them through action.

You want people to feel valued, appreciated, and involved. Doing so increases your ability to move barriers to new ideas and improves the speed and flow of change.

SELF—PROMOTING, POOR COMMUNICATORS, WON'T SHARE INFORMATION

Howard Hughes was born in 1905 and inherited a fortune from his father, who had invented a pivotal oil drilling drill.

He is noted for his contributions to the film industry and aviation. He produced and directed big-budget films, including "Hell's Angels," a World War I epic. After forming the Hughes Aircraft Company, he also set multiple air speed records.

He developed a reputation for perfectionism and being a visionary, which helped and hindered him in his business career.

In 1939, he acquired a controlling interest in Trans World Airlines (TWA), where he oversaw significant growth and expansion.

They became known for the levels of comfort and technological advancements in their aircraft, and they were the first to offer transcontinental flights across the US.

However, his style was not conducive to ongoing success.

He was somewhat of a recluse and indeed suffered from mental health problems.

He tried to impose unilateral decisions on the business without consultation and frequently conflicted with the executive board.

He was also known for his indecisiveness, which led to significant delays in the introduction of jet aircraft during the 1960s—a crucial time for airlines as they battled to accommodate the increasing number of passengers.

His style led him into several drawn-out legal battles in the company and with the US Government until, in 1960, a court decision forced him to relinquish his control over TWA, marking the end of his direct involvement.

Through his vision, he transformed TWA into a major international airline and set new standards for the industry. However, his inability to cooperate with others and to communicate led to the company being left behind as technology advanced and to personal conflicts with those around him.

There is often value from people who are independent, self-motivated, visionaries, but there is a line that, when crossed, damages the performance of the team.

Difficult people can present themselves as talented but unwilling to work with others, set aside their agenda, and share information and experience for the good of the whole group.

A team should be greater than the sum of its parts, but someone who is uncooperative, uncommunicative, and unwilling to share information can damage the team regardless of their abilities.

This can be even more pronounced in teams of talented people who see little or no value in cooperating.

No matter how great, their talents do not add up to the total value that could be expected if they did not operate in such a difficult manner.

Are you part of a team? Do you prioritise the group's success over your own personal success? Does everyone else?

When I arrived at the Wigan RLFC training ground at Robin Park in 1993, it was a hot, dry, sunny afternoon. At the time, it was an athletics track, with the pink running track set against a stand on one side and a wide space of green fields at the back.

Today, it is the home of the new modern stadium of Wigan Warriors, a fully professional team of athletes who remain dominant in the sport, 30 years after I was a player there, a testimony to their methods.

In 1993, the team was recognised as the most professionalised squad in the game, but it was a pioneer. The majority of players were not full-time professionals in rugby league.

Rugby League is a working-class sport mostly played in towns across the North of England, Australia, New Zealand and other South Sea Islands.

A poorer relation of its more illustrious brother, Rugby Union, it has long struggled for the same audience globally and in England.

Supporters are passionate and committed, amateurs play a thriving junior game, and players, supporters, and officials argue endlessly about its greatness. Perhaps even thriving in the position of largely ignored and unknown sport compared to football, rugby union, and many others.

In 1993, professional players were paid, something only recently introduced in Rugby Union, but they were not paid full-time in most cases. Match fees were paid to teams who were victorious. Otherwise, the money was barely enough to cover travel expenses to train.

The pay rate for winning was based on the team's level, the fixture's importance, and the wealth of the club's benefactors, who generously financed the game.

This meant there was fierce competition to rise to the top and play regularly for the top teams in the big matches.

Showpiece finals such as the Challenge Cup Final played at Wembley Stadium in front of up to 90,000 supporters, the Premiership Final played at Old Trafford, Manchester, to a crowd of 60,000 fans, and critical derby matches could earn a player thousands.

The staff and senior players at Wigan RLFC in the early 1990s set a new standard of professionalism in terms of training, conditioning and systems.

They worked hard to end the traditions of heavy drinking, lack of personal strength and conditioning, and teams that relied on individual brilliance to win matches that had dominated for decades.

They introduced personalised training plans and six-day-per-week training sessions, including conditioning, skills, and organisation drills. They also created a club playbook with match strategies and player roles consistent and understood by all 50 squad members across three teams.

The goal was complete interchangeability, where any player could easily slot into the system in any team, making development faster and the loss of players through injury less of an issue.

That afternoon, when I arrived at Robin Park for the first time with my training boots in hand, I was joining my first session in a gruelling 12-week pre-season programme that was mandatory for all players.

I stood around with the other men, some of them household names outside of Rugby League circles, such was the team's dominance in the 1990s. Players like Martin Offiah, Shaun Edwards, and Jason Robinson arrived to join the session.

That day, the squad went inside for some circuit training, a series of exercises for 30-second blocks in sequence before heading outside into the sun to perform interval sprints.

It was intense and hot. As we jogged to the start of the intervals, we took off our shirts, exposing glistening muscles covered in a sheen of sweat.

The challenge was to sprint around the edge of the large field outside the stadium between cones. There was limited time to arrive at the next cone, and any spare time was spent resting. We set off again at full speed to the next cone a few seconds later.

So it continued for what seemed like forever, but was probably about 20 minutes.

Afterwards, exhausted, we split into groups to begin skills drills that lasted another hour.

It was like nothing else I had encountered.

As the programme evolved during the following 12 weeks in the build-up to the season, it continued much the same way, except that groups were formed.

These groups made up the three squads of players for the upcoming season: the first, reserve, and development teams.

Competition was fierce because your place in these teams dictated the money you could earn and the recognition you would receive from supporters.

Your performance depended on financial success and status as a legend within a town that believed in the sport as a second religion.

I noticed something rather interesting.

There was a strong camaraderie across the squad as a whole, friendship groups and lots of laughter - perhaps the shared suffering helped bond us, but there was a queer sense of mistrust.

Despite the stated intention to play a certain way, an unselfish strategy designed to exploit the weak points in the opposition's defence, there was a reward for non-compliance.

A report in the local newspaper describing a score that a player achieved through an act of personal brilliance created tempting recognition.

Coaches at the end of matches congratulated players who had been successful despite not adhering to agreed-upon tactics.

Players were incentivised to discard the strategy to serve their interests, get noticed, progress, and earn more.

Reflecting on this time, I feel frustrated by my naivety.

I was used to clubs, school and friendships that were always reciprocal.

I found myself following the rules because that was necessary for all of us to succeed. I had been drilled to understand that teams win together and lose together.

I even started to change how I played the game to fit into the game plan and listen to the coach's feedback.

I was used to operating freely, using my speed and elusive skills to pass opponents and find space.

On one occasion, during a cup semi-final at Halifax, a small town in West Yorkshire, I received a kick from the opposition. I picked up the ball, skipped past an opponent close to the sideline, and ran 20 metres, putting the team on the front foot for the next phase.

I received a message from the coach on the sideline, warning me that I was close to the edge of the field and risked losing the ball.

I took this to heart and found myself playing ever more within my capacity, when instinctively I understood that greatness exists on the edges.

Others did not follow such feedback and were rewarded.

It was my first experience of such a situation, which taught me much.

Years later, I came across something similar in a business that openly promoted values such as teamwork. Managers recognised one of the key values each year as a key part of the ways of working at a prize ceremony and were awarded with a trophy.,

However, it was obvious that teamwork was not rewarded day to day.

The people noticed by the business acted in their own interests first, withholding information and not communicating.

There was an active incentive to reward salespeople who stood out through their own actions and to create a sense of competition across the regions, which meant it was not in your interests to share information.

Top salespeople gained access to a network of customers through relationship building. There was no incentive for them to share how they had achieved success because doing so would create greater pressure to deliver more the following year.

The business and the rugby club were cultivating a culture of people who were incentivised to operate alone, withhold information, and not communicate with others.

Perverse Incentives

When the British Empire ruled India, people naturally feared snakes. There are no very poisonous snakes in the British Isles, and as such, we have no idea how to avoid them, find them, or deal with them in the countries that we visit.

In Delhi, there was a problem with cobras.

The British rulers feared them and wanted to rid the city of their menace. To solve the problem, they offered a financial reward for every dead snake delivered.

Ingenious locals saw the obvious business opportunity.

They began to breed cobras, and then, once mature, would deliver them, dead, to the authorities in return for the bounty.

It wasn't long before the governors understood what was happening and cancelled the reward.

Suddenly, with no reward for their work and the obvious risks of breeding poisonous snakes, the locals who had been making money cast out their snakes into the streets, leaving more snakes in Delhi than before the bounty was launched.

The incentive had been perverted into something that delivered quite the opposite of what was required.

I was once told by a leader that "You get what you measure"

It was completely true and remains so.

People are eager to please and want the rewards that come with success and achieving goals.

There is a temptation to measure the outputs of actions; after all, the outputs deliver value.

A sales organisation prioritising sales results drives its teams to secure sales at all costs. Indeed, many industries focus on significant bonuses as the main source of income for sales teams and risk unethical or illegal behaviours to secure the results.

A TV series called "White Gold" aired several years ago.

It was the story of a salesman who, in the 1980s, sold double-glazing doors door-to-door. His rewards for securing sales were significant, and he had plenty of opportunities to win business.

Political changes at the time meant a vast increase in home ownership in the UK, and with it, the value of investing in security and heat retention for homeowners. Suddenly, there was a reason to spend money on new windows: homeowners would increase the value of their assets.

It was a perfect storm for poor behaviour. Salespeople have the reason to push sales aggressively, and homeowners have the reason to spend money.

The series followed the main character as he used tactics designed to pressure potential buyers into closing a deal, including refusing to leave their home until they agreed, regardless of how late in the evening it became.

Another example is the rewards available to bank traders. In his book The Trading Game, Gary Stevenson, a former foreign currency trader at Citigroup, describes how bonuses work.

He explains that once traders earn the right to their own book of business, they are rewarded by a bonus calculated as a percentage of the profit they earn for the bank during the year.

Salaries are high compared to many other industries, but pale into insignificance when compared to the potential bonuses that traders can earn.

It encourages risk-taking and discourages collaboration with other traders since bonus pots are limited and larger shares are awarded to top performers.

Explore Motives

Reflect on the difficult people you have encountered who fit into this category of poor communication, self-promoting and refusing to share information. What are they trying to achieve through their actions?

What are they rewarded for both intrinsically and extrinsically?

At work, we are often seeking tangible rewards for our hard work. We want to secure a promotion to a role with more responsibilities, gain a pay increase, achieve objectives, and secure a bonus.

We also seek less tangible rewards. Many people want to be recognised for their intellect, noted as leaders, and talked about as people who deliver results and can be trusted to do what is necessary to achieve outcomes.

The phrase "we get what we measure" helps us understand why difficult people behave as they do.

These difficult people are likely doing what they are supposed to do to progress.

A personality driven by an emphasis on results can easily find themselves working in ways others consider self-promoting, uncommunicative and refusing to share information when they are recognised and rewarded for doing so.

When large groups of people behave this way, it is a sign of an imbalanced culture that is moving towards losing the importance of relationships.

The result will likely be groups of individuals who operate alone, view others with mistrust and hold knowledge as evidence of personal power and status.

Rewarding Collaboration

To change this kind of culture, the way that people are rewarded must shift. When you get what you measure, you need to measure things that are genuinely contributing to the success of the group as a whole and not recognise individual contributions too much.

Sales is a classic dilemma in this context.

There is often a correlation between the number of customers seen by a representative and the sales that are delivered as a result. Therefore, it can make sense to measure the number of customer visits and reward this measure as an interim indicator of upcoming performance.

This is useful during long sales cycles or when a few high-value sales take time to close.

The difficulty is that rewarding the volume of meetings ignores an important element of sales performance, which is the quality of those meetings.

Many poor-quality meetings or meetings with the wrong type of customer will not lead to better results.

It is much more important to focus on measuring what truly matters to the business, create fewer and even shifting measures, and reward teams and groups for performance rather than individuals.

John Doerr's book Measure What Matters delves into the concept of OKR as a tool for aligning goals throughout the organisation and focusing on short, medium, and long-term goals that directly contribute to the business's performance.

In his book Winners, Alastair Campbell explores the power of objectives, strategies, and tactics as leadership tools designed to create clear, unified direction for diverse teams in politics and sports.

These inspiring works help us understand the key role of setting direction in unlocking performance and driving the right behaviours.

Managers are equipped with the tools to align actions to performance, review progress, and take action against people who are not working with others to deliver results.

I worked with a client some years ago operating in a highly competitive marketplace with tiny margins.

As a family-owned wholesale business, they forged a strong reputation for customer service and personal experience, which was a strong point of difference. However, they struggled to deliver results and maintain growth in a market where price dominated customer discussions.

The owners recruited people to make outbound and manage inbound calls to customers, selling business and taking orders. They also managed larger customers themselves while trying to find new business opportunities and being creative with what they had.

Together, we invested significant time creating and crafting objectives throughout the business.

We started at the highest level, discussing the business objectives themselves and working through the leadership team, finance team, warehousing, sales and customer services.

During the discussions and debates, I noted two key factors that would drive future business performance, but if left ignored, would make little difference to the day-to-day.

These are the high-value but hard-to-do tasks that many businesses forget about because they take time, are difficult to measure in a year, and are complex.

It is easy to focus on the short term, reward delivery and worry about the future another day.

In this case, I urged the team to address them.

One was a complete refresh of the warehouse computer systems, and the second was opening up a completely new customer channel.

A medium-sized wholesale business relies on its ability to manage stock to compete. Its range can never match the largest suppliers. Instead, it needs to be smart with stock management to reduce stock holding costs and sell what is profitable and what drives volume.

A stock management system that integrates with finance and sales systems can be an essential asset, but it is expensive to buy, complex to install, and disruptive. Because of its cross-functional nature, it is also outside the scope of any single role in the team, meaning there is no obvious owner.

A new customer channel is a similar challenge. Little is known about the market, the buyer needs, the products that must be sourced and stocked, the supply chain and delivery to customers, and the customer base itself.

Everything needs to be constructed from scratch. This takes time and investment, which businesses already stretched by day-to-day pressures and cash flow limits cannot afford.

However, if a team can unlock these opportunities, they become future growth and profit opportunities that few competitors can match because of the barriers to entry.

I spotted these opportunities, and we set out to create the objectives that would deliver them.

Everything was aligned through the Managing Director and his direct reports so that the short-term targets of the business and the long-term strategic levers were specified.

The team courageously embraced objectives, strategies, and tactics, setting the stage for a clear business transformation.

Star performers left the team because they didn't like the new way of working. It wasn't that the business wanted them to leave, but they saw from how they were being managed that the old ways of working alone, not sharing information, and not communicating, were not welcome.

Instead, the team encouraged sharing, collaboration, and the fact that many objectives were entangled with others in the business meant that they had to communicate.

It took over three years to complete, but the Sales Director launched a new customer offering to a new business sector that had been developed, researched, tested, and expanded. He created a strategic partnership with a large customer, someone who would benefit from the offering but was also prepared to be a test bed in return for a share in the sector.

A few months later, the new warehousing system was launched to a company-wide fanfare.

The team successfully collaborated to deliver two complex projects over several years, which have the power to protect jobs for everyone long term.

Addressing self-promoting, uncommunicative people who won't share information requires a clarity of goals that measure and reward not individual performance but group performance. These goals must align throughout the business to avoid perverse incentives, and they must be supported by a management framework that focuses on collective performance.

It also needs to be understood that these difficult people might be delivering exactly what is expected of them. We must notice what that is and what they desire, and make sure we direct their energy most productively.

POLITICAL, AUTHORITARIAN & DOMINANT

Kevin Spacey is an outcast today because of his alleged inappropriate behaviour towards others and allegations of sexual misconduct. Still, in the past, he was recognised as a brilliant actor and has won many awards.

The first time I saw him in House of Cards, the show totally gripped me, and I was hooked on the series.

The series follows his character, Frank Underwood, who was Secretary of State in the US Government and rose through the political system to become President of the United States.

Some of the series' magic comes from Frank's occasional turn to the camera and direct communication with the audience watching at home.

The first time he did so, it took my breath away.

He includes us in the drama as it unfolds, sharing his thoughts and plans like coconspirators.

We witness what is happening, and his engagement with us changes our relationship with the character from casual observers to allegiance.

This is a difficult place to be because Frank is a diabolical person.

He is obsessed with power and will go to any lengths to accumulate it.

During the series, we witness him using blackmail, threats, intimidation and murder.

He abuses people, conspires with others, plots, and schemes. His only loyalty is to himself.

Frank throws a journalist in front of a train in one of the most famous and shocking scenes at the start of the second series.

During the first series, Zoe and Frank create a symbiotic relationship. She is given access to information that she can use to build her career in return for her favour in writing stories that benefit Frank and his rise to power.

But she becomes a problem for Frank through her questioning and challenging ways, refusing to bow down to him. He becomes angry and pushes her in front of a subway train, killing her.

In a shocking scene, afterwards he speaks to us, the audience, while standing at his bathroom mirror and urges us not to "...feel sorry for Miss Barnes, because every kitten becomes a cat"

Frank is a classical Machiavellian character. Obsessed with accumulating power and using devious, manipulative and downright evil tactics to get it.

His character is aggressive, authoritarian and dominant. He uses charm when necessary, but just beneath the surface lurks a cold, calculating, selfish personality that drives him relentlessly.

The House of Cards series was a global success, running for 5 years and attracting millions of viewers.

We are attracted to Frank Underwood's evil, malignant character. Something fascinates us about someone prepared to do anything to further his own success.

But when we meet these people at work, they are anything but fascinating.

These can be toxic individuals who destroy company culture and damage trust, but they are rarely as obvious as Frank Underwood.

In 2022, Elizabeth Holmes was convicted of wire fraud and was sentenced to 11 years in prison.

She was the founder of Theranos, a company that claimed to have invented a blood testing machine that would revolutionise patient testing.

The promise was that the machine could identify and diagnose a whole series of diseases by analysing a single drop of blood.

The potential was enormous.

It could revolutionise disease screening in the developed world, streamlining testing and increasing diagnosis rates. It could also transform the developing world, reducing healthcare costs for patients and providers.

Her company and her products created significant excitement among potential customers and investors, who kept investing in a company destined to deliver incredible results.

Elizabeth Holmes was a skilled communicator, strategist and visionary.

However, she also lacked empathy; she was manipulative and calculating.

Her ability to convince seemingly smart and experienced investors to invest in the business is still largely unexplained.

She was able to secure funding from some notable names, including The Walton Family, founders of Walmart, who invested $150 million, Rupert Murdoch, the media mogul, who invested $125 million, and Henry Kissinger, former US Secretary of State, who invested $3 million.

Elizabeth Holmes became famous for being the youngest self-made female billionaire. At its peak, the company was valued at $9 billion.

She was charismatic and persuasive, which she used to secure investments from notable people. She was also known for her style, sporting a black turtleneck.

In her talk at TEDMED, a health event associated with TED, she gave a powerful speech on Theranos's vision and shared a personal story from her childhood about an uncle who died from cancer.

From the stage, her vision to diagnose disease before symptoms appear is delivered with calm sincerity. She communicates authority in her all-black attire, commands the stage with confidence and poise, and engages the audience.

But there was no machine.

Theranos was a fraud.

Her employees describe her life working at Theranos as one where she created a culture of fear. She engineered an organisation shrouded in secrecy, and it was little wonder, given that she was hiding the fact that the machine she was supposed to be ready to launch did not exist.

Employees who raised concerns about the technology and how the business was run were singled out, treated badly, and fired.

Elizabeth Holmes used her charisma to manipulate people around her and rise to Silicon Valley's top.

She built political allegiances with people who became intertwined with her success and who, through their investments and public endorsement, needed her to be proven right or risk personal embarrassment.

She was relentless in her ambition and would stop at nothing to achieve her goals.

Today, she continues to protest her innocence from prison, claiming that the technology's problems were typical start-up challenges and were not a deliberate attempt to mislead investors.

Political Authoritarian and Dominant People Around You

I have heard many conversations over the years referencing certain people within a business who are the political operators.

We notice them because they support leaders, regardless of the circumstances.

It is almost irrelevant what the topic is; they are aligned with the boss, and they are vocal about it.

I saw this in action several years ago at a client meeting. I was lucky enough to be invited to join a multi-day event with a client to help me connect with key people I would be working with and better understand the team's priorities and strategies for the year ahead.

We were in a beautiful hotel in the city centre, close to Madrid's bustling streets and coffee shops.

The whole leadership team was in attendance at the event because they were hosting a series of presentations and workshops to guide the group through the intricacies of the plans for the coming years.

I noticed that one team member was incredibly vocal and supportive of the executive vice president of the business.

When the EVP made a point, he was the first to affirm statements with positive encouragement, and at one point, he started to deal with some of the questions coming from the group on behalf of the senior leader.

At a coffee break, I asked some of the team about who he was and what his role was. The responses astounded me.

His role was not especially clear. He had worked for the EVP in a previous position and had been brought to the team as a project manager and execution expert.

He had almost no commercial experience, with no history of sales, marketing, or finance. He had joined the business in a project delivery role. He had accompanied the EVP through the organisation in ever-increasing grades, with more responsibilities and power, but little evidence of distinct performance.

Moreover, it was understood that nobody should challenge or cross him because he was known to be vindictive, negative and conspiratorial.

There was widespread fear that he had the power, connections, and influence to damage careers and perhaps end them.

Some people within businesses invest their time and resources in cultivating relationships to accumulate power and influence rather than delivering against company objectives.

They often operate in a highly directive style, telling people what to do and using the strength of character and force to gain compliance.

When questioned or challenged, they can react defensively, becoming animated and aggressive, often taking questions personally and responding in a personal manner.

Many tasks must be completed when preparing for a complex negotiation with a government.

With one client, we were required to construct a presentation summarising the key points of our proposal to deliver to a negotiation committee.

Following this presentation, there would be a series of negotiation meetings that could result in a deal that could be worth billions of dollars to my client.

As is normal for these types of deals, the stakes are high, and there is a strong desire for people to want to be involved.

The agreement's legacy can last for years and make or break careers.

We sat around a table with an extended team of people discussing the negotiation team and the various roles required to represent the cross-functional group and secure the best deal.

The leader of the business unit stood up and glared around the table.

He met the eyes of everyone in the room before launching into a tirade.

He had heard that people were bidding for a place in the negotiation team, and he was furious. He bellowed around the group that "I am in charge of this team and I will decide who sits at the negotiation table and if I hear of anyone going behind my back, there will be hell to pay"

I was stunned.

It is rare to see this type of reaction, and I immediately noticed the style and recognised the personality.

Personality Traits

So far, my description of these people suggests a group of extremists dominating meeting rooms around the world, but that is not necessarily the case.

These people are difficult because although they are ambitious, they are charming and able to connect with key people and create alliances.

They build associations with people they recognise could help them and absorb some of the power from these relationships to help them.

In contrast to the previous chapter, where difficult people used isolation to help them, these people do the opposite.

They assess the organisation's politics and work hard to become part of the decision-making groups.

While working at Roche in the UK, I was part of a business unit specialising in bone.

It was a unit in its infancy, but I was not part of its birth and joined a few years later.

The business unit had two key products: a treatment for osteoporosis, which was anticipated to be a leading brand and could secure significant volumes at relatively low prices.

It was part of a joint venture agreement with GSK, where the sales and marketing teams worked together to bring the product to market. As a result, it was part of a global structure spanning both companies.

The second brand was a more specialist product, a monoclonal antibody used to treat arthritis.

Again, part of a joint venture deal was a more straightforward agreement based on sole responsibility to market the product in certain regions. Roche owned the rights to Europe and was able to make unilateral decisions.

As a specialist brand, this product did not require significant field force resources. Few customers treated arthritis, and these could be visited by a small group of specialist experts supported by a marketing and communications team at head office.

The osteoporosis treatment was very different.

There were potentially tens of thousands of decision makers, including primary care physicians, hospital doctors, and many across specialities.

This product presented an opportunity to build a significant business unit infrastructure, including dozens of people, associated budgets, and prestige.

When Roche began the journey into bone health, the person responsible for the osteoporosis brand was a very junior, but ambitious lady.

She had only a few years' experience in the industry, and she quickly spotted an opportunity.

The allocation of resources and budgets was very closely associated with the brands' sales forecasts. The more ambitious the forecasts, the more resources are needed to deliver the results.

Companies are prepared to invest in a brand in its infancy. Furthermore, executives welcome aggressive forecasts because they boost good news stories and eventually share values.

Issues arise when these forecasts are not delivered, but this happens several years after the initial promises are made. Leaders who have made the promises have often moved on and do not have to bear the consequences of overforecasts.

In the case of Roche, the junior brand manager made some incredibly aggressive forecasts for the brand's success.

She worked with her joint venture partners at GSK, and they were able to gain agreement that these forecasts were acceptable. Why not? It was in everyone's interests to be positive, ambitious and aggressive.

As a result, she created a situation where Roche had no choice but to recruit an extended marketing group with enough people to support this mega brand. They also needed to expand the sales force and create a more significant presence in the market with the associated sales leadership.

At the heart of it all was the originator, the visionary who, through her relationships with Roche executives, had positioned herself as the natural business unit head despite her relative inexperience.

I joined the team just over 2 years later when the brand was in trouble.

Sales forecasts had failed to materialise, and something radical needed to happen.

Roche recruited a talented and experienced team to work on the brand. We had market experience from various competitor brands, and our team leader was a talented marketer and leader with intimate knowledge of the joint venture partner, GSK.

In turn, GSK switched around their team and brought in new faces to reinvigorate the business.

We adapted the marketing plans, repositioned the brand, and created strategies to incorporate changes to the customer's decision-making processes.

But to little avail.

A change in sales trajectory was insufficient to cover the gap between expected sales and current best-case forecasts, and the businesses made some tough decisions.

GSK decided to exit the joint venture agreement in the UK, and Roche made significant changes to the business structure. As Roche slashed jobs to save costs, all the marketing roles were at risk of redundancy.

The lady who had started it all was still leading the business unit, but in her new expanded role, was accountable for both brands and not for the day-to-day operations.

She shifted from someone making forecasts to someone reviewing and approving them, in partnership with executives at Roche. She was able to move the accountability for failure to hit targets to market forces, poor performance across the joint venture and other factors, such that she retained her status as a prestigious business unit leader in one of the most successful pharmaceutical companies in Europe.

Difficult people who are political, dominant and authoritarian exist in subtle forms.

They build associations that enable them to take challenging positions against others in the organisation and thus exert power.

This power can be seen in group situations when they want to represent 'leaders' in their opinions and are prepared to speak on others' behalf as executives' voices.

They are vocal, ensuring they are heard during meetings, especially when an audience of senior people is present to witness them.

I have noticed they are prepared to make statements to an audience that they do not necessarily restate in personal meetings without the audience. In smaller groups, they can be much more reasonable and flexible.

They are ambitious, both for themselves and for the departments that they represent. Ambition helps them attract investment, gain support from others in the business, and accumulate authority.

Indeed, they are often more ambitious than average on aspects such as performance targets because doing so attracts positive attention from more senior people who hear what they want to hear regarding forecast results.

Unlocking Their True Intentions

What is driving the person who is political, authoritarian and dominant?

The simple answer is power.

We are communal animals and function best in groups. Throughout history, we have banded together to overcome obstacles, build great civilisations, invent incredible technology, and flourish.

Our instinct to work together and collaborate is so strong that many of our heroes are people who have achieved incredible feats alone.

Take Felicity Aston, for example. She is a polar explorer and Antarctic scientist.

In 2012, she was the first person to ski across Antarctica, travelling over 1,000 miles in 59 days. During the challenge, she spoke of the challenges of complete isolation.

She described that once you leave the coastal regions of Antarctica, there is nothing at all, not even wildlife and that can become a very otherworldly experience.

Within a few days, Felicity started to doubt her memories and could not imagine a world outside of where she was right at that moment.

During snowstorms, a regular occurrence in Antarctica, all the senses are completely numbed. There is nothing to see except white; there are no smells, no sounds, and nobody to talk to. This played tricks on her mind, and she imagined a variety of sights and sounds simply to fill in the gaps that her brain had from the lack of stimuli.

Another problem was that she had no inspiration, no one to motivate her when it was cold, and she was exhausted.

It would have been so easy for her to listen to the nagging voice in her head urging her to pitch a tent, get warm, and rest because she had done enough. Without colleagues to challenge her and keep her going, she had to rely on tenacity to keep going.

Operating alone creates many physical and mental challenges because we are not designed to do so. This is why we admire people like Felicity so much: They go against our natural inclination to work together.

Loneliness has long been something to fear and has frequently been used as a punishment.

Throughout the ages, incarceration in solitary confinement has been used as an additional level of punishment.

We need people, family, and community in order to flourish, belong, feel safe, and succeed.

Denying ourselves these things is torture, punishment and challenging.

This is significant because as we evolved as community animals, we were safer when living in groups. We could rely on others to help us find food, build shelter, and protect us from predators.

We could share information on the location of food sources and the best way to build a shelter from harsh weather. We passed on skills like fire-building and hunting techniques, and this ability to share information meant that every generation could build on the skills of the last.

To be cast out of the community meant almost certain death.

It would mean losing the ability to reproduce, pass on genes, and share our hard-earned knowledge and experiences.

Therefore, many of our basic instincts are designed to help us remain part of the community. We are empathetic, reciprocate favours, and develop complex verbal and nonverbal communication techniques to connect with others.

One of the additional aspects of this communal living is understanding the role of hierarchy in the community.

The more senior we are in the community, the more we are entitled to its privileges. We get first choice in available food, we can choose with whom to mate, and we are given safer, more protected spaces to sleep.

As such, in addition to our instinct to become part of a community, we also have a powerful urge to rise to higher status positions in the group.

We witness this urge with difficult people who are political, authoritarian and dominant.

They are trying to rise through an organisation through political associations, a tried-and-tested strategy, and then use this authority to protect themselves from challengers.

Challengers could be others who are also trying to rise through the ranks and displace them, but they can also be people who expose a lack of credibility or experience.

An internal fear of being exposed as incompetent could be a powerful motivator.

We witness once again the twin motives of towards and away from motivation. We see people here who are trying to gain power and authority, but may also be afraid of losing status and respect from others.

Their behaviours, challenges, demonstrations of power, associations with high-status people, and dominance could be manifestations of a need to gain more power and protect themselves.

Elizabeth Holmes dropped out of Stanford to concentrate on Theranos. This is a well-known part of her story, and she shared it actively to try to demonstrate her commitment to the business and perhaps emulate others, such as Steve Jobs, the founder of Apple, who didn't finish college.

But it could also have created a sense of inadequacy that she was determined to protect. She was aggressive in challenging people in the business who questioned her; perhaps she was worried that they would see something she was afraid to share, some inadequacy, something that would reduce her credibility.

The boss I worked with at Roche certainly acted this way. She was reluctant to engage with the team, and I had few conversations with her during my time there.

We once spent 10 days in a strategy retreat with our joint venture partners at GSK, debating and discussing how to turn the business around. The whole GSK team was there, but our leader was not.

Succeeding with Political, Authoritarian and Dominant People

There is a very real danger that confronting this type of person will trigger a power struggle that could drain your personal resources and damage your relationships.

You are going to create factions in the business, asking people to take sides, support you in your struggle, or choose this other person. Even if you are successful in challenging them, there will be consequences for morale and culture.

There is also an important question to consider.

What does success look like?

By challenging this personality, what are you expecting to achieve?

You might successfully get them to back down on a particular issue, but what about the next issue?

This is not a person who will change their personality due to something you say or do, or because they were unsuccessful on a particular topic. They see this strategy as a method of building power in the long term and perhaps overcoming some particular shortcomings concerning skills or experience.

The best approach to deal with this difficult person is to start by exploring their relative power and making some courageous decisions.

Often, we credit others with more power than they really have.

It is easy to imagine, especially because this person will encourage it, that this person has significant power and influence over decision-makers. Consequently, we imagine that they can destroy our reputation or career with a single word.

This is rarely the case.

On a less emotional level, we are making some huge assumptions from this belief.

We assume that the people this person will speak to trust them entirely and will not rely on their judgment or consult with anyone else before deciding to block our career.

We also assume that we are so important to them that they will invest their resources in blocking our progress, rather than other agenda items they might have.

A more balanced view suggests they are not all powerful, and we can overcome their difficulties.

Furthermore, we are underestimating our levels of credibility and influence in the business. It is important to trust ourselves and our skills.

Succeeding in overcoming these people as difficult colleagues requires us to find ways to form alliances, especially on certain topics.

If we can become someone they see as advocates, then we are no longer a threat but an asset.

I had a client experiencing issues with this type of person in her business. My client felt that everything she did and said was questioned by this personality; she could not get them to respect her and became increasingly frustrated at being made to feel small during leadership discussions.

What changed things was a shared belief in the importance of women as leaders.

Both these people were women, and they worked in a male-dominated business.

My client raised the shared goal that, as the only two women on the male-dominated leadership team, they should jointly campaign for greater presence across the business.

They aligned perfectly on this topic, and the previously difficult person started to use her weight and influence to support my client.

Based on this person's recommendation, my client was encouraged to apply for a new role with a higher grade and greater responsibility.

The alliance was built from a shared goal into their general relationship and created a sense of shared accountability for change.

Overcoming difficult people like this requires a style of relationship jujitsu in which you use their power as an asset.

Fighting back will become exhausting and damaging. Instead, you should choose to understand what they are trying to do and find areas of shared goals.

Avoid exposing their weaknesses, as it will likely be a sensitive topic and elicit an emotional and defensive reaction.

If they have little experience in marketing and you speak to them about how you can help them with marketing, they could feel threatened.

If they are dedicated to detailed operational issues, you can agree with them on the importance of getting things delivered.

You are likely to need to be humble but not subservient. They want to associate with people who have power; those who do not have it have no use.

In that case, you are building your credibility as an expert, which will draw them towards you, as long as you don't push against them.

Talk about how you can deliver great things together and how important alliances are for you and the team. Speak of using different strengths to contribute to the whole performance.

When you see issues with their ideas, raise these questions in personal meetings and exchanges, rather than in public. Their public persona is important to their status and authority, and to be questioned creates risk for them.

These people can be influenced through small changes they can own over time. They will align with the prevailing ideas. Their potency comes from creating leverage over others through arguments, force and alliances.

By gradually changing the tone, you can remove these, make them an ally, and get them to use their influence to support topics important to you. This will avoid a clash with this difficult personality.

LESSONS FROM DIFFICULT COLLEAGUES

As part of negotiation workshops, I often run an exercise which is set from the perspective of an internal negotiation. The people at the workshop are usually from the same organisation, so it echoes closely their reality, working with colleagues to negotiate a problem.

During the exercise, some people in the group will act in their own self-interest. They will be more demanding, less flexible, and less willing to share resources and make selfish proposals.

Afterwards, during the learning and discussion, it becomes obvious what has happened, and frequently other members of the group are shocked and angered that colleagues could behave that way.

They feel angry that someone could behave so selfishly, take advantage of them, and outright lie to further their personal ends.

But this is the reality.

Organisations reward people who stand out because of their performance goals. The rewards take the form of promotion to higher grades, increased salaries, bonuses, recognition and access to senior people. In summary, increased power and wealth.

With such incentives at stake, it is little wonder that people behave selfishly.

Rewards are limited, and businesses structure themselves to limit access to these rewards to the few people whom they believe deserve them.

There are powerful towards motivations, things to gain and potent away from inventives, fears that drive behaviour.

When you add to this cocktail the variety of ways that we interpret the world, personal ways of working and communication styles, it is little wonder that we find difficult colleagues in various forms.

We have explored a variety of personalities in this chapter from people who act in siloes, people who are negative, people who won't share information and people who try to dominate through power.

They are all seeking the same goals. They all want to gain recognition, status, rewards and success.

This is how businesses are structured, and understanding is the key to succeeding and outsmarting difficult colleagues.

It is not enough to assume that because you work in the same company and with the same overarching goals, you should be working together.

The competing agendas are the personal goals and the company goals. The elephant in the room with difficult colleagues is often that they place their personal goals ahead of the company, or at least they are not willing to sacrifice their personal agenda to put the company first.

They protect information, create siloes, and act the way they do because they are convinced that doing so will give them an advantage.

They are not trying to be difficult; they are trying to succeed, and they are using strategies that they are convinced will be effective.

Your challenge is to understand their goals, not the tangible goals of the business, but the emotional goals that are truly the motives for action.

When you understand these, you are more able to draw boundaries that protect you from exploitation and better outsmart them by helping them minimise their fears or work towards their goals.

Commercially and personally, we are all seeking tangible and emotional goals. The companies we work for are a means for us to achieve these objectives of security, income, status, and belonging, and they are powerful incentives for action.

Do not believe that because you share the same company, colleagues should all act selflessly; they will not.

Difficulties arise when their agenda conflicts with yours, and unpicking that is the secret to outsmarting them.

SECTION 03:
DIFFICULT MANAGERS

2011 saw the release of the movie Horrible Bosses. The story, a black comedy, follows three friends who are fed up with the behaviour of their abusive bosses and plot to murder them.

They suffer the humiliation of sexual advances, sadistic and torturous behaviour, threats and incompetence.

It is a dark and comedic exploration of the lengths people might go to escape from the tyranny of an awful boss.

Our bosses play a critical role in our work experience. Hundreds of books explore the factors of great leadership, some of the world's leading business schools teach leadership, and dozens of training programmes are available to help us become better managers.

Yet, poor management and leadership continue to plague us in business.

Great leaders inspire us, challenge us to improve and bring groups together in very special ways.

Poor leaders can ruin careers, divide groups, destroy relationships, and create enormous stress for their teams.

In this section, we will explore some aspects of poor managers' behaviour, uncover their motives, and share ideas that help us succeed despite them.

INFLEXIBLE, TASK FOCUSSED & DISMISSIVE OF PERSONAL ISSUES

I am intense when it comes to focusing on a task and getting things done.

It is not uncommon for me to work 14 or 15 hours a day, and I focus hard on creating and delivering high-quality content for my clients.

I am the same when it comes to my personal life.

In December 2023, I was experiencing some challenging times and decided to focus on my health and fitness.

I chose a series of interesting audiobooks, including Never Finished by David Goggins, The Brothers Karamazov by Fyodor Dostoevsky, Humankind by Rutger Bregman, and The Laws of Human Nature by Robert Greene, and I set up a plan to listen to them.

I made the choice that if I could watch TV for an hour a day, I could go for a walk. But if I were going to walk for an hour, why not run?

Using that logic, I ran 10km daily for almost 2 years.

I worked my way through a series of audiobooks and competed in 2 marathons and several ultra-marathon events.

The only thing that stopped me from continuing that way was increasing pain in my thigh as a result of scarring from serious knee surgery when I was in my 30s, after I snapped my knee ligament.

What I did during that time was normalise the abnormal.

Since then, I have spoken to others about the experience and offered my advice as they face various challenges.

I understand that we must make choices when we commit to achieving something. These choices require us to sacrifice something in order to pursue our objective.

In my case, I chose to stop watching TV and accept that, at whatever time I had available, from early morning until late at night, I chose to run.

I felt all the effort was worth it.

I saw no real sacrifice. I did not miss TV because I became immersed in wonderful books and stories, and got very fit.

But I am also very lucky.

I have very supportive people around me and am flexible enough to get up early and go out late.

I live in a good part of the country with access to a river and pathways, and I am fit enough to challenge myself in this manner.

Not everyone is as fortunate as I am, and that is where I am understanding.

My choices to avoid TV and prioritise my work allow me to write material, respond to emails, think, create notes and record content throughout the day and the weekend.

I commonly go to my office for a few hours during the weekend to focus on a particular task when others might choose to go to the pub.

Because I am working, my clients and colleagues will receive messages from me at all hours of the day and night and on the weekend.

I don't expect replies.

I am not Elon Musk.

The Tesla Model 3 was launched in 2017 to global acclaim and marked a significant milestone for Tesla.

Their previous models were designed and launched as exclusive luxury cars. For Tesla to be taken seriously as a mainstream vehicle manufacturer, the Model 3 needed to be a success.

It was their opportunity to offer an affordable electric car, costing around $35,000 at launch, and scale up manufacturing to deliver cars for the mass market.

In doing so, they would transform the electric vehicle market into a serious market to compete with the established brands, catapulting them to global domination of an emerging and exciting category.

They were also very ambitious with the design, aspiring to create an advanced vehicle with an innovative touchscreen interface and autopilot capabilities.

The Model 3 was a key milestone in dealing with the environmental challenges of petrol cars, making electric cars a viable and aspirational alternative for the global market.

The pressure on the team was immense.

They needed to create aerodynamic, efficient, lightweight prototypes before dealing with significant production issues.

Producing prototypes is relatively easy with attention to detail and engineers poring over every aspect. Production at scale is a different level of complexity.

Building factories, setting up machinery, sequencing production, finding efficiencies and increasing the production rate without risking quality are enormous barriers.

Tesla's CEO, Elon Musk, chose to sleep on the factory floor while the Model 3 was being developed.

He tried to prove to the team that he was willing to suffer with them to deliver the desired result. He wanted to be on site immediately to address questions and work through problems, and he set a high standard of dedication to the team. They witnessed him working hard to meet the production targets they were chasing.

However, Elon Musk's choices to focus on the targets he had set were not optional for his team.

Famously, Elon Musk makes unforgiving demands of his people. He requires that the team work into the night and over the weekend to meet the deadlines.

He is known to fire employees he does not believe are dedicated or hard working enough.

Two weeks after he purchased the social media giant Twitter, now named X, he sent an email to the remaining workforce telling them that they were required to work in a more hardcore way and complete long hours at high intensity.

As a result of his email, it is estimated that hundreds of staff members resigned.

There is a specific leadership style that is described as task-oriented leadership.

It is a prioritisation of hitting targets as the primary focus of activities. These managers communicate clear objectives so that everyone can understand and work towards delivering these goals.

They establish clear processes that need to be followed to drive efficiencies, perhaps limiting the amount of time available for specific delivery stages.

I have several connections who work in the fashion and entertainment industries. These are incredibly fast-moving businesses that require their teams to be able to deliver creativity, but to industrialise it.

They are very clear about the stages of the creative and development processes, but they also limit the time spent on these steps.

To invest too much time at this stage risks the overall efficiency of the process at the cost of diminishing additional value, which is how they justify the choice to move on as quickly as they dare.

Finally, task-oriented leaders have a rewards system that incentivises and recognises the delivery of these targets.

Part of the start-up culture in California's technology industry is a share of the company's eventual success through shares.

Employees dedicate long hours, evenings, weekends and significant amounts of energy and passion to the business in return for stock holdings that they can sell when the company eventually goes public, providing them with what they hope to be life-changing amounts of money.

Timothy Sehn is a good example of this phenomenon. He was Vice President of Engineering at Snap Inc., Snapchat's parent company. Responsible for the app's development, he held shares worth $165 million when the company went public in March 2017.

These incentives can be powerful motivators to work within an intense culture of task leadership.

It is not just a phenomenon of technology companies from the US.

Telesales and contact centre workers often experience this kind of culture.

They are given challenging targets to meet each day. There are high expectations for call volumes answered and dialled, sales targets that are tracked hourly and weekly, and a demanding culture driven by managers and leaders who track activity every minute of each day.

This environment has no space for flexibility and empathy for personal issues.

All that matters are the results today, and people who fail to meet the standard are judged harshly.

I worked with a client who sold software solutions to the contact centre industry in the UK and the US. Through working closely with the team there, I started to understand the existing structure and pressure for target delivery.

Efficiency is the name of the game in contact centres. The leadership constantly balances the demands of customers making calls to the centre with the available resources.

Customers who make calls to a contact centre, like any of us trying to speak to a customer service agent at our bank or phone provider, do not want to wait too long in a queue.

They also want to be able to send emails or join live chat.

The company needs to have the resources to answer calls, handle emails, and manage chat, but if it has too many people available, it will spend too much money and be judged to be wasteful.

The businesses employ talented analysts who use complex models and software to predict demand on any given day and match resources to demand.

For the mathematics to work, they need to model the expectations for how much work each of their agents can cope with in an hour.

The higher the agent's output, the fewer are needed, and the more efficient and productive the centre becomes.

In this environment, it is easy to understand why personal mobile phones are often banned from agents' desks. You can see why toilet breaks are timed and monitored, and you can recognise why managers spend as little time as possible training, supporting, and talking to their team.

Instead of briefing meetings and coaching sessions, messages pop up on the screen with instructions, and face-to-face events are kept short, with directive speeches.

But it is also understandable why contact centres have an incredibly high staff turnover. In the UK, the turnover of staff can be as high as 30%, placing it towards the top of a league table that employers are unlikely to want to win.

Managers who operate this way are dedicated to the task at the expense of the relationship because they see the business's role as a task-oriented element.

They see the business as the job and the job as the task.

The space for personal issues is non-existent.

This culture is connected to a view of capitalism that goes back generations. It is believed that the role of the business is to drive shareholder value, in the form of share price, at the expense of everything else.

Indeed, CEO of large companies are frequently remunerated in the form of shares, and as such, their incentive to increase the share price is a personally motivated one to increase their own wealth.

It can incentivise short-term tactical approaches to business, where the share value over the coming 90 days is the most important factor. Any view of long-term investment is a risky approach that could tempt the wrath of the board.

I often find it amusing to read global strategies penned by CEO and Senior Executives that include the importance of shareholder value as a key driver of performance because of the direct connection to their income.

CEO's are significant shareholders in the business and are often rewarded through the allocation of more shares. When they are challenged to grow share price, they are directly increasing the value of the assets that they are being awarded.

Could you imagine agreeing to an objective with your boss that directly increased your salary? How might they react?

This is common in sales where objectives directly connect to bonus payments, but many other departments do not have such a clear connection between action and income.

When CEOs do it, we accept it as part of business culture despite the side effects of creating a short-term, dismissive, task-focused organisation that does not allow space for personal issues.

What is Gained from this Approach

In a world where significant cultural capital and power are associated with the accumulation of wealth, there are obvious motivations for operating as this kind of leader.

Indeed, a cycle powered by a desire to increase personal wealth and power could drive behaviours that make these aspects central to decision-making.

If the value of personal relationships, empathy, and kindness is believed to be low, and the value of wealth, success, and power is viewed as high, then people seeking power could be encouraged to focus on tasks at the expense of relationships.

Intellect is also highly valued over relationship management skills because of the perceived benefits that high levels of intelligence bring to a business.

Problem solving through detailed analysis of complex situations and identification of solutions is a key example of this focus on intelligence. There is also a reliance on innovation in businesses, and with technology playing a leading role in the highest value organisations on the stock market, the value of people capable of creating intellectual property is high.

The stock market worldwide is dominated by brand names such as Microsoft, Apple, Google, Tesla, Facebook, and Amazon. All businesses are founded on the creation and exploitation of technology.

An additional group of powerful businesses, such as NVIDIA, which creates the microchips used by these leading companies, is a recent addition to the elite.

For decades, companies have traded on the creation of intellectual property in healthcare.

Pharmaceutical companies that develop and launch medicines and vaccines, created by brilliant minds and marketed worldwide, have consistently driven innovation.

Not to mention companies such as Samsung, Sony and LG, which engineer televisions, music systems, and video recording technology.

Innovation, problem-solving, and strategic thinking are highly prized assets for companies worldwide in the race to dominate their markets and deliver profits.

This unrelenting focus on the importance of intellect for business is underpinned by academic systems that reward and recognise research and results. From a young age, we are conditioned to the status associated with academia and encouraged to study, improve our test scores, and be seen as intelligent.

Warren Buffett, CEO of Berkshire Hathaway, is regarded as one of the most successful investors of the last 30 years. He has amassed a huge personal fortune of over $150 billion, and his investment company is valued at over $1 trillion.

He values intellect over everything else.

He believes the intelligence to make smart decisions is the foundation of business success.

He tempers this belief with the need for integrity and ethical conduct, knowing that intelligence without these traits can lead to unethical behaviour.

A person who is dismissive of personal relationships, inflexible, and task-focused could view themselves as intellectual and smart.

They could prize these traits at the exclusion of others and relentlessly focus on delivering results.

They may be someone who strongly emphasises the importance of dedication and hard work for success.

Indeed, many successful business executives place hard work at the centre of their success.

Melanie Perkins and her husband founded Canva in 2013. They wanted to democratise design, making it simpler and more accessible to users.

The marketplace for graphic design was already competitive, with organisations such as Adobe, Microsoft, and Pixlr already fighting hard for share.

Her vision was to reach beyond professionals in graphic design and expand use to everyone. Her challenge was to create a system that was intuitive to use, had the same high-end features as the professional software and scale the business.

Today, Canva serves 130 million monthly users, and its freemium model appeals to millions of everyday users who can create designs for use at schools, clubs, and teams without the expense.

She had often spoken of the importance of hard work to her success. She set herself 'crazy big goals' and worked tirelessly to achieve them.

Hard work and dedication can distinguish between good and great, or success and failure.

In his book 'The Talent Code', Daniel Coyle explores the myelin theory of skills development.

Myelin is a coating that surrounds nerve cells, and it becomes thicker and more efficient the more we practice a particular skill.

Coyle argues that excellence in any skill comes from thousands of hours of dedicated practice. This dedicated practice builds myelin and pathways that become stronger and stronger, enabling us to become highly proficient.

I am of the age where typing was a skill I needed to develop after I left school. Unlike today, keyboards and computers were not regularly used during my studies. When I was given my first computer at work, aged 24, I had almost no typing experience.

I agonised over the keyboard each day, trying to tap out emails and fill in reports for the business. I knew I could write much faster and make fewer mistakes, but I had no choice.

After decades of practice, I instinctively know where letters are positioned and can type confidently, reasonably fast, and accurately.

This is the theory of myelin in action.

Over time, my repeated effort to find keys has resulted in an unconscious knowledge of where they are and how to tap them correctly to write a message.

This theory of hard work delivering rewards provides hope for many of us who feel it is an opportunity to outshine our more intellectual competitors.

The rationale follows that if I am prepared to work harder and with more dedication than someone else, I will prevail even if they initially had more talent.

Together, these beliefs can provide a powerful motivator to focus on the task at the expense of relationships and flexibility.

A belief that success is a result of intelligence and not relationship building, combined with the belief that hard work delivers results, creates a personality that behaves inflexibly towards colleagues.

These are the beliefs of Elon Musk, and as the richest man on the planet, he provides a powerful role model for many.

Dealing with a Relentless Manager

If I am honest, this personality is the one I most identify with.

I am a hard worker. I value people around me who are willing to put in hard work. I know how important it is to me because when I encounter people with a different approach, perhaps a more relaxed attitude to work, I find it hard to understand and frustrating.

I know people who put in as little effort as possible. They are focused on the minimum of tasks required to avoid difficulties, and they focus on time, working the minimum hours required by the business.

I cannot identify with this attitude at all.

I have always taken incredible pride in my work, and since I was 18, I have filled my days with productivity and effort.

I chose a science degree at university. At the time, I was only interested in playing rugby; it was my passion, and I had a wonderful opportunity to make a career of it after signing a professional contract with the leading British team.

My parents forced me to make a trade-off by requiring me to attend university at the same time. For them, education was essential, and they saw sport as a pastime and of little value otherwise.

They said sport was not a way to make a living, and I needed qualifications.

St Helens was a town built on heavy industry, and in the 1990s, the jobs there were dominated by those that paid a weekly wage. Many people I went to school with began working in tyre centres or apprenticeships on building sites.

These were good jobs, but my parents wanted more. They wanted me to secure a job with a monthly salary and benefits, a job that did not operate week by week.

The only way they would support me signing a professional sports contract was if I also agreed to go to university simultaneously.

At school, the subjects that I enjoyed the most were sports and sciences. I loved learning about how things work, especially biology.

This led me to conclude that the best subject to choose at university would be science-based. So, when I received my somewhat disappointing grades on leaving school, I was offered a place at Liverpool University to study biomedical science.

This was a mixture of various sciences connected to medicine and, depending on choices, could lead to honours degrees in biochemistry, biology, anatomy, pharmacology and others.

To me, it sounded perfect. An interesting topic and close to where I wanted to be located.

What I did not fully understand at the time was the time commitment compared to other choices

My degree required attendance at 2 or 3 lectures each morning and participation in 3 or 4 afternoons per week doing practical work.

That meant most days were full attendance days. On top of that, I was expected to be at team training sessions 3 times per week, attend gym sessions 2 or 3 times per week and prepare for match day, which could be Wednesday, Friday or Saturday.

It was a big commitment, and I would wake up each morning, drive the 50 minutes to university in Liverpool, spend the day there, then drive directly to Wigan for training before returning home about 8:30 pm. At that point, I would eat and do the required study before going to bed.

I got into the habit of relentless work from the age of 18, and it stood me in good stead during my career, where I have continued to work harder than average in my pursuit of goals.

Early in my career as a salesperson, I discovered that most people are lazy and do not do what they are expected to do. They seek shortcuts and hacks that enable them to do less.

I understood that if I was prepared to do the fundamentals, I would be ahead. For example, if we were supposed to meet with three customers per day and I did so, I would be ahead of the competition because most people didn't do it, believing they could 'get away' with doing less.

But one of the biggest lessons I learned from this time at university was the importance of focusing on performance.

I was trying to do everything, commit to a challenging degree course, play top-class sports, and maintain some sort of social life. I learned it was impossible.

On reflection, I was not fully committed to anything, especially sport, which at that level cannot be done without full dedication.

With hindsight, I should have waited to go to university. Universities have existed for hundreds of years, and students arrive every year to complete their courses. It has been almost 30 years since I left university, and the University of Liverpool remains a respected institution.

Sport provides a unique and timely opportunity. These moments are rare and fleeting. If things didn't work out, it would have made much more sense to focus entirely on it and attend university 1-2 years later.

By making this choice, I could have focused on excellence in one area, knowing that this level of dedication would reap its own rewards.

In this context, we can understand how to succeed with managers who are dismissive of personal issues and task-focused.

They see only the job at hand, and as such, you need to focus on that topic.

They respect people they judge to be hard working and feel contempt for people who try to take shortcuts, don't put effort in or seem distracted by other elements.

They do not see why they should sacrifice their business performance because you want to spend the afternoon at your son's school sports event.

They do not empathise with you because you want to be home in time to share dinner with your family if you have important work to do.

What they might respect more is framing these elements as contributing to your focus on excellence at work.

They want to think you are as dedicated as they are, and you need to demonstrate that you are indeed a hard worker, prepared to put in the hours.

If you want them to demonstrate flexibility, you need to explain how it will help you to be more productive.

If you want to be home for dinner with the family and that requires you to leave the office at a set time, explain to them that you are most productive when you operate according to a schedule.

You develop detailed plans that map out strategies to be most productive. At work, that means you set tasks and schedules, create focus time, and deliver projects. But you also apply the same principles to your personal life, and as such, you commit to protected time.

What that means for your business performance is that you can focus long-term on productivity because you have a balanced life, where you spend time working and spending time with others you care about.

In this case, you are not asking for flexibility or for them to consider your personal situation; you are, in fact, setting high standards of scheduling that you apply to all aspects of your life.

I am a hard worker and look for others around me to work hard, but I also need them to be productive and have space to recover.

Recovery is a well-researched aspect of sports performance, and even in 1990, massage was advised as a way to relax and recover from intensive training.

Business is no different, and today, many tools and techniques are used to provide space to recover from intensity.

A manager obsessed with hard work and performance must also respect the time for recovery.

You must ensure that you have completed the hard work before expecting space for recovery.

Many of these personality types recite the mantra " Work hard, play hard," but both must be present.

You do not need to work to the same standards that they have, but they do want to witness your efforts.

I am fortunate that because of my business, the extra effort I put in is rewarded with the progress of the business, assuming I am doing the right things.

The same is not always true within a corporation, when income is limited and promotions are managed.

However, you can work hard within the boundaries, earn your manager's respect, and use this respect to your benefit when you want some flexibility.

A client of mine switched their sales channel from face-to-face to telesales after the COVID-19 lockdowns in 2020.

It was a strategy to reduce costs under intense pressure and to maintain some customer connections when meetings were impossible. Still, they decided to continue it long term because they saw no long-term sales impact, but retained the lower operating costs.

During the switch, they also noticed an increased frequency of contact with customers.

With fewer people, they could make more phone connections to customers than the team on the road.

Part of this realisation came from the sales team no longer need-ing to drive between customer visits. But it was also because the telesales team were more visible and it was harder for them to waste time.

The initial plan was to retain the same salespeople where possible and protect the relationships with customers, but over the following few months, nearly all of the sales team left.

They didn't like the visibility, scrutiny, or hard work. They valued driving around, coffee, and long, meaningless customer conversations.

On the surface, it could appear that my client implemented a task-based leadership approach, removed flexibility, and disregarded relationships, but that is not true.

They did increase the sales team's expectations of customer contacts compared to previously, but they retained the atmosphere of flexibility.

In return for delivering call volumes and meeting quality standards that could now be more easily monitored, they offered rewards, recognition, bonuses and flexibility.

If you are willing to respect the beliefs of a task-based manager, you can work in a productive and rewarding environment. You just need to draw your boundaries and deliver results.

MICROMANAGERS WHO DISEMPOWER AND REFUSE TO SHARE RECOGNITION

Sales is a special function because it combines the ability to connect with people, build trust, understand their problems, and build relationships with them. It also combines the ability to share technical information and work through a process that ends in a completed deal.

There are many ways to succeed in sales, and despite the research, nobody has been able to define the perfect personality for sales.

Nobody has achieved this, possibly because customers are so different. When dealing with different personalities and needs as customers, we need different personalities from salespeople.

There are dozens of sales processes devised and hundreds of books describing ways to progress and close deals. Some are very industry-specific, and others are broader, but they share something in common: they do not prescribe the exact things to say.

I read The Challenger Sale by Brent Adamson and Matthew Dixon and found it interesting and useful. In the book, they explore a variety of personality types with the intention of researching which personality type is the best for sales. They identify several different personas: the relationship builder, the lone wolf, the hard worker, the reactive problem solver and the challenger.

The research concluded that the challenger personality type is by far the most successful when it comes to solution sales. In the book, they characterise this person's traits and explore how they are more able to navigate the ups and downs of the market than the other styles.

They do not explain exactly what to do and say to be a challenger. They broadly describe what is required and how companies can build a challenger culture, but stop short of creating a script.

To me, this tells a clear story about empowerment in sales.

Sales success demands a high level of personal accountability. Nobody can tell us exactly what to do to close a deal. There is a lot of advice, coaching, structure, and process, but ultimately, the intimacy of human interaction between seller and buyer and the situation that surrounds them define the deal.

Salespeople are judged on their results. They close enough deals to justify their position, or they need to explain why they are failing to meet objectives.

Accountability lies squarely with the individual, and that is something that I find attractive about the profession. We are trusted to meet with customers and close agreements on behalf of the business. It is a privilege to be responsible for income, and few enjoy it.

In 2008, I joined GSK in a marketing position and started to hear more about empowerment across the organisation. Because of my experience in sales, I found this confusing.

I remember sitting in a conference centre at an airport hotel near Heathrow for a business meeting. About 100 people were there, including all the UK commercial marketing and sales leadership.

We sat around tables in a cabaret style with a smart branded notepad and pen in front of us, listening to the UK Executive team lead us through a series of workshops exploring values, culture and performance.

It was an excellent chance for me to meet new colleagues and hear first-hand about how we were expected to work.

GSK had a relatively new CEO at the time, Andrew Witty. The UK business was very proud of him because he had started his commercial career in the UK team as a graduate trainee, and several people in the audience knew him as a junior colleague. Imagine the feeling of nurturing a junior staff member who would soon grow to become the CEO of the entire global business.

One of the buzzwords Andrew Witty often used in his addresses was the need to increase empowerment within the organisation.

He recognised the experience and knowledge of people throughout the business and wanted them to feel able to make decisions.

He wanted to ensure that decisions were taken quickly, locally, and promptly to make the business more agile and dynamic.

The problem was that the more he spoke, the more everyone wanted empowerment.

He failed to define empowerment, create a boundary for it, or describe the types of decisions that people were empowered to make.

Empowerment is a confusing term.

I know many leaders who want their teams to be empowered because they understand the team's knowledge and experience and want to unlock it.

The difficulty they have is that they are also very smart people, with great experience and knowledge that they want to use.

In addition, many beliefs about leadership are that we direct and instruct people.

This creates a tension.

Is it possible to empower a team and be a manager with power? I think not.

If you imagine power as a glass full of water standing on the corner of a leader's desk, this provides an illustrative way to demonstrate the challenge of empowerment.

The cool glass of water sits there, with drops of condensation gathering on the glass and running down the side onto the leather place mat.

It is waiting for the manager to use whenever they want to implement a decision in the business. During a meeting or discussion, when asked for their opinion, the leader can reach across to the glass of power water and use some of it to get their way.

It encourages the team to approach the manager when they need a decision.

It creates a situation where the manager becomes a critical central point for choices. They are involved with all the key decisions in the business, they have visibility of everything, and their opinion truly matters because they are the ones in charge of the cool and potent glass of power water.

When a manager empowers their team, they must give them some of the water from the glass.

If the water is the power source and the person who has it has the power, then it is only possible to empower someone by giving them some water.

When that happens, the manager will have less water and therefore less power. Here lies the biggest challenge for managers who want to empower their team.

They cannot keep their power and empower others; there are choices and trade-offs, and these choices mean that leadership loses control of decisions, loses visibility of options and needs to trust their teams to make smart choices.

The benefit of empowerment in a business is a dynamic organisation that is quicker and more nimble in decision-making, hence the attraction for Andrew Witty. However, it also creates a completely different role for leadership.

Margaret Thatcher, the Prime Minister of the UK from 1979 until 1990, was well known for her strong and directive leadership style.

She was the leader of the Conservative Party and the first female prime minister. During her time in leadership, she regularly took a strong stance and was highly directive.

She had a clear vision for how she wanted the UK to change and what she wanted to achieve, and she believed that it required her to be clear, uncompromising and direct in order to deliver change.

She wanted to act fast, make quick decisions and hold very strong beliefs, leading her to operate the way she did. She was dedicated to the idea that her politics were for the next generation, not the next election, and therefore prioritised the long term over the short-term politics.

I grew up in the North of England during her domination of British politics, and my earliest memories of the Prime Minister speaking were listening to her strong voice, shouting down objectors, and using her force of will to gain agreement.

In 1980, Margaret Thatcher negotiated with US President Jimmy Carter to purchase Trident Nuclear submarines.

This was a headline that I remember dominating the news for many years, such was the controversy surrounding it. I had no idea of its significance, but with hindsight, it provides an insight into her operating style.

Trident was a set of nuclear submarines armed with nuclear weapons that were part of a nuclear deterrent against the Soviet Union.

The deal to buy the submarines cost the UK economy the equivalent of £24 billion today. It was taken without consultation with the rest of the Cabinet, including the Defence Secretary John Nott.

The cabinet was against the purchase because it did not believe that it was strategically necessary or that the deal represented value for money.

It is a perfect example of how Margaret Thatcher did not empower her team to make decisions. She felt keeping the power for herself was faster and more appropriate.

Indeed, her uncompromising approach and unforgiving standards would often bring her into conflict with her team. Norman Tebbitt, a loyal supporter of Margaret Thatcher, was frequently in conflict with her because of how he described her tendency to belittle people around her.

This aspect of leaders who refuse to empower their teams is important for understanding them as difficult managers.

Standards of Excellence

A manager with very high standards of excellence and a clear definition of what and how to deliver these standards could find it hard to empower the people around them.

If their experience delegating tasks to colleagues results in quality that does not meet their personal expectations, they feel disappointed.

That disappointment can fuel a lack of faith in colleagues' ability to deliver the expected results or do so in a way they feel is expected.

The cycle that results from this experience is that tasks are delegated from the manager to the team member, and the manager is unhappy about the completed work and feels they could have done it better themselves. Therefore, in the future, the manager will refuse to delegate tasks.

I have struggled with these feelings in the past.

Several years ago, I was encouraged to take on a personal assistant.

Like many business owners, I was running my business alone, which meant managing business development, finance, invoicing, emails, events, technology, website, subcontractors, and more.

I had adopted a series of tools to support me in my daily activities, such as Calendly, which I used to manage meeting bookings, but I was very busy.

A friend challenged my thinking. She questioned whether the cost of paying someone to take on many tasks was the same as the cost of doing these tasks myself.

It was a great question, and I realised that the income from my focusing on key tasks was much greater than the cost of outsourcing certain elements to someone else.

Therefore, I found a personal assistant to support me day to day.

The biggest barrier I faced, though, was outsourcing the tasks!

On many occasions, I believed that the time required to explain what I wanted to do and how it should be done to someone else was greater than the time it took me to do it myself.

Since then, I have spoken to others about their experiences, and they recount similar tales.

Indeed, when I speak to agencies that provide resources such as outsourcing personal assistants, they raise the same challenge. Clients are unable to deliberately leave tasks to people they are employing to take on certain aspects.

The problem is a bias towards the short-term view of productivity.

It reminded me of a story told by my Economics teacher when I was 13.

I chose to study Economics at school. It was in the same options group as History and Geography, and in those days, I had little enthusiasm for them, but Economics appeared to be a new and interesting subject.

The lessons were held in the school's computer room. At the time, we had only one room full of computers, and people didn't really know how to use them!

We sat at desks facing the wall away from the teacher. The room was full of computer equipment, such as keyboards, mice, and screens. There was little space to work, and the whole room was impractical for a standard subject.

I remember little of what Mr O'Neill taught in that class except for the computers, the fact that Margaret Thatcher resigned during one of the lessons, and a story he told about investments.

He told a story about a man who was shipwrecked on a desert island. The man crawled to the shore from the might of the open sea and climbed to safety on the rocks.

There he finds a pool full of little fish. The man realises that with effort and persistence, he can catch enough fish to keep himself alive, but only if he tries all day, because the fish are very hard to catch with his hands.

He recognises that he could stay there, just about living on these fish, but life will be a struggle.

His alternative is to sacrifice and take a risk. The man could suffer for a day, go hungry instead of catching fish, and risk finding some materials on the island with which he can build a net.

With the net, he could catch more fish more quickly, and the extra energy and time he saved could be used to find more resources, build a shelter, and create a long-term plan.

The story illustrates the value of short-term sacrifice, investment of time and resources, and risk-taking for long-term prosperity.

When we constantly view tasks through the present lens, we miss the value of investing in the future to create greater freedom.

It is this insight that fuels the thinking and behaviour of managers who are unable to empower their team and recognise the skills that they have.

They might believe that they are more skilled than their team members and that the team is unable to deliver the same standards. They could think that their skills are impossible to teach in a reasonable amount of time and that they need to get the job done now.

They are perhaps operating in a short-term mindset, driven by near-sighted goals and the performance in the next quarter.

We explored this issue earlier concerning the lack of balance in performance, which is driven by the need to meet short-term targets.

Managers who do not empower their teams and do not recognise the talent that exists there are worried that they are the only people they can trust to get things done.

They might also have a lack of confidence.

It takes self-assurance to hand over power to team members and recognise their excellence levels.

Managers who fear they will be overtaken by more talented people are more likely to resist offering these people autonomy in case they are successful, and that success overshadows the leader's abilities.

A fear of losing status through team members who are more capable or a fear of losing status through team members who are not capable would fuel similar behaviours, reducing the incentive to empower and recognise the skills of others.

Overall, managers who do not empower and recognise others will likely lack trust in their capabilities, fear losing status, or fear not delivering results.

Building Trust

Trust can and needs to be earned when managers do not empower teams. We will explore trust in more detail later, but it is critical in the context of managers who refuse to empower the team or do not recognise capabilities.

One of the important elements of trust is reliability.

When we trust others, we become increasingly confident that they are reliable and consistent in their actions.

If my daughter goes out with friends for a quick dinner or drinks and tells me that she will be back in a few hours, I am confident and trusting that she will be as good as her word, if she has proven to consistently do as she promises.

If one evening she fails to show up as promised and forgets to send me a message telling me what has happened, then I lose faith in her word.

Our level of trust depends on the history of our relationship. If the first time I trust someone, they let me down, then all trust is gone, and it is very hard for me to trust them in the future.

If we have a long-standing relationship and they disappoint me much later, I can remember the many occasions when they were consistent, and I can forgive them.

Unlocking success with difficult people requires us to understand their fears and address them in our behaviours, adapting to account for them.

A manager who does not trust the team, as we have explored, is likely to be afraid that they will be disappointed by their actions.

They could fear being embarrassed by what the team says or does. They might worry that poor results will affect their business and reputation, and they could fear poor choices reflecting badly on them as leaders.

But how can you earn trust if they do not trust you?

One aspect requires us to be courageous in our relationship with the manager. We need to challenge them to let us participate in the task. If we are completely excluded, then there is no opportunity for us to learn and develop.

Once we have addressed this issue and been given access to the planning and delivery of the tasks, we can prove that we are capable through our contribution.

Over time, through evidence of our calm, considered, careful, and respectful behaviour, we earn increasing levels of trust and freedom to work alone.

We give our managers the confidence they need to empower us to act and earn any recognition they give us.

Not long after I secured my first full-time position in sales, I was transferred to a new team with a new manager and a new sales geography.

It was less than a year after my first contract position, which was a huge change for me. I had new products, new customers, a new manager, and new colleagues.

I felt apprehensive. This was not something I wanted, and it turns out that my new manager felt exactly the same way! She didn't want me either.

It was normal and encouraged for managers to shadow the sales team, and she immediately arranged to spend a day with me and my new customers.

We met at a supermarket car park in the morning, in time to share a coffee and discuss the plans for the day. It was as we sat at the plastic table, drinking supermarket cafe coffee, that she explained how the day would work.

She explained that she would lead the conversations with my customers as the manager because I needed to prove that I could lead the conversation myself. Only then would she trust me with the conversation.

I was shocked.

I understood my inexperience relative to the rest of the group, but I was confident in my capabilities to influence and connect with customers.

I also had a degree in pharmacology and understood the medicines and disease areas we would discuss.

She totally disempowered me and did not recognise my capabilities.

I sheepishly stood up and we went to the car to drive to my first meeting of the day, wondering what this day would be like.

We arrived at the office of my first meeting about thirty minutes later and waited to be invited in to talk with him.

We walked into the meeting room where two doctors sat. I sat opposite them with my manager on my right. She introduced herself, I introduced myself, and the meeting began.

I started to talk about our products; I asked some questions of the doctors. My manager stepped in and asked some more direct questions, questions that I did not like, because they were leading questions typical of salespeople who are not genuinely curious, but are seeking the 'right' answer, so I stepped back in.

I felt my heart racing as I did so, uncertain of how my manager would receive this. I didn't look at her, just in case, but I could sense her looking at me.

I pushed on and handled the rest of the meeting, explained the products, and we discussed the pros and cons, ending with some actions to follow up.

Afterwards, we sat in the car, I in the driver's seat, which turned out to be prophetic. She accepted that I had done a decent job on the call and was OK with me continuing that way.

I felt justified, but our relationship was damaged, and we never got past a feeling that she didn't want me in the group, and she was forced to take me, and the fact that I didn't want to be there.

I left a few months later.

It was a low point in my career, but there were important lessons about courage, respect and empowerment.

As a manager, I understood the importance of supporting team members' confidence in their ability to succeed, empowering them, and gathering evidence of their capabilities.

Managers who do not empower or recognise you have no evidence that you are up to their standards.

It is up to you to prove that you are and earn their trust.

Find ways to demonstrate your capability through preparation and practice. Ensure that they know you want to reach their standards, follow their guidance, and deliver results for them.

The value of a team is the ability to deliver more than individuals can through collective action. Managers who do not empower or recognise others take away this power, but simply focusing on that will not be enough to change their minds.

That ignores their fears that you acting independently will result in greater, and perhaps immediate, losses.

They require proof, evidence of consistency and acknowledgement of their need for results that reflect well on them.

You must also understand that they will always save much of the power for themselves.

A major frustration at GSK when Andrew Witty launched his empowerment drive was that everyone seemed to want the power for themselves. This is never going to happen; power and the scope of decision-making will always be limited in different parts of the business and must be earned over time.

Disempowering managers need to feel empowered themselves, and the amount they give you will be limited. Over time, you can earn more freedom. My boss, who didn't trust me, did trust some of my colleagues.

One of them was trusted highly to work almost as an equal to her. He earned that right over time, through patience and evidence of consistent results.

CREATE A CULTURE WHERE PEOPLE FEAR MAKING MISTAKES

In 2006, I left sales and moved to a marketing role at Roche's head office. It was my first office-based role, and I had no idea what to expect.

I went to the office just outside Welwyn Garden City in Hertfordshire for an interview and was impressed by the building. I could imagine myself working there. I liked the vibe—it was cool and chic, unlike buildings I had visited before.

It was a modern building with glass-fronted offices along a long corridor. Set on three levels, it had a cafe, a coffee shop, a gym, and ample parking.

The parking was relevant because the office, situated on the same business estate as Tesco, was over 50 miles from home and would require me to drive every day.

Travel was going to be the biggest barrier to my success in this role. I needed to be in the office every day from 9 a.m. to 5 p.m., which was something new.

It would be expensive because I also needed to buy my first ever personal car, having them provided for me previously as part of a job package in my sales roles.

This was especially complicated because my children were very small at the time, so a family car was necessary.

In the next few years of office-based work and long commuting, I became increasingly aware of the need for an economical, fuel-efficient car, suitable for the family and reliable enough to drive 500 miles per week.

I started to look around, and of course, a Volkswagen diesel car kept coming up repeatedly as an ideal choice.

Volkswagen had a reputation for reliability, excellent build quality and value for money.

They had also become well-known for developing much cleaner diesel engine technology.

The late 2000s and early 2010s were a time of growth for the business, driven by CEO Martin Winterkorn's ambition to create the biggest car maker in the world and government pressure to move to clean diesel and reduce toxic emissions.

The UK government offered lower tax charges for cars that could meet lower emissions standards.

What nobody realised at the time was that Martin Winterkorn was leading a toxic work culture that resulted in the installation of technology in cars that allowed them to cheat emissions tests.

When tested, cars that demonstrated low emissions of toxic substances were, in fact, emitting the same levels of toxicity as standard diesel cars.

It was a huge scandal which resulted in significant financial implications for Volkswagen and criminal charges against CEO Martin Winterkorn.

But how could it happen that such a large organisation was prepared to install technology into cars to knowingly cheat environmental standards?

The answer was the culture created from the top, a toxic, autocratic and aggressive culture.

Martin Winterkorn's vision was to triple US car sales and crack a notoriously challenging market. He also wanted to do so with a focus on diesel engines rather than the hybrid market. In the US, diesel-engined cars represented only a small part of the market, around 5%, so he was trying to crack a competitive market in a demonstrably hard-to-sell segment.

It is difficult to see how Volkswagen could have taken on a more difficult challenge, and it placed enormous pressure on engineers to invent the required technology.

The leadership involved themselves in even minor decisions, creating a culture in which colleagues were afraid to admit mistakes or contradict managers.

Bullying engineers and firing executives who displeased him became almost a badge of honour. Winterkorn wanted to hear only positive progress, and an industry analyst noted at the time that teams made sure they had good news before reporting to him.

The solution that engineers delivered for Volkswagen was not an efficient diesel engine with low emissions; it was one that cheated the emissions tests in the US by recognising test conditions and altering performance to meet standards.

In road conditions, the car emitted toxins at a scale 35 times greater than the limits.

When the scandal broke in 2014, there was a huge fallout. Martin Winterkorn resigned, and senior engineers were suspended or put on leave, and Volkswagen halted the sales of its 2015 models.

Where is the line between a strong leader chasing an ambitious vision and an authoritarian tyrant who frightens their staff?

Information is power. The more information we have about a topic, the more confident we become in our assessment of the challenges and in our ability to find answers and solutions.

Information is a protected resource in negotiations, and negotiators are careful about how much they reveal to the other party because of its association with power.

If you have few alternatives to an agreement and do not have the budget to buy a competitor, and the other party learns this information, they have significant power in your agreement because they know your limitations.

However, information is not static; it evolves and changes over time as options develop.

A failure to evolve and adapt to new information becomes an Achilles' heel for leaders.

One of the major differences between autocratic rule in business and visionary leadership is the response to new information.

One afternoon, a colleague called to warn me about a potential problem with a client I was about to meet with.

I was in a meeting room at an event, laying out my notes, plugging in my laptop and pouring myself a glass of water as the phone rang.

My colleague explained that some senior executives from the leadership team of our client company had just met with one of the senior leaders from our business to discuss an ongoing contract.

Our client, one of the largest and longest-standing, had made some suggestions to our team about how they would like to change how they work.

Although they intended to continue the partnership, they asked for some important changes to how solutions were delivered. They wanted less reliance on costly hotel conference facilities and more flexibility in scheduling to accommodate their workforce.

It was reported to me that our senior leadership were incensed!

"How dare you tell me how to run my business?" I was told that was the reaction from our team, and the client had not received it well.

My colleague wanted to warn me ahead of the event so that I could respond to any comments that might be made.

This is a great example of a leader who becomes obsessed with their ways of working and fails to adapt to changing needs.

There are dozens of examples of companies that were fixated on their existing business model and did not adapt to new technology. A frequently cited example is the contrast between Netflix and Blockbuster Video's fortunes.

Blockbuster dominated home movie rentals during a time when we owned DVD players and could call into a store, collect a movie to watch over the weekend, and return it a few days later.

Netflix, in contrast, offered a postage service for DVDS and evolved to a model of movie streaming, even before most people had rapid internet connections at home.

Blockbuster had the opportunity to buy Netflix at an early stage and adopt its technology. Still, they also had access to information about changing consumer habits that they could have used to inform their strategies

They did neither.

Over time, Blockbuster became increasingly irrelevant, and Netflix was founded and dominated a new market segment of subscriber-based streaming services.

Leaders who are insensitive and create a negative culture of fear are often fixated on their mission and do not accept new information.

A dogged determination to build something visionary and transformative motivates and inspires them, and it can be initially infectious. However, they fail to absorb new information and feedback, which frustrates and damages the people around them.

Focus on What & How

One of these people's difficulties is the oversimplification of visionary leaders from the past.

Nelson Mandela is a great example.

Mandela was imprisoned for many years for his role in objecting to apartheid in South Africa and being a member of a designated terrorist organisation, the African National Congress (ANC), but he remained a relentless campaigner despite his imprisonment for 27 years.

Following his release in 1990, he continued his mission and was unflinching in his resolve to bring change to the country and to realise the dream that all South Africans could live together in peace and equality.

He was elected the first black president of South Africa in 1994 to global acclaim and began rebuilding the country using his vision.

It's an inspiring story. A man unwavering, unflinching, able to suffer humiliation and hardship in prison for nearly 3 decades, ultimately realises his vision and unites the country.

It could be seen as a perfect example of laser-focused and immovable leadership.

However, Nelson Mandela had a vision that engaged and inspired the people around him to find solutions to problems and work through details.

He changed his approach and shifted away from his controversial violence connections to engage and inspire people in a positive way.

He used the skills of other leaders of his party, the African National Congress (ANC), to negotiate with former adversaries.

His vision of equality for all races demanded that the minority ruling white class were not now discriminated against but was engaged in the transition.

South Africa is a complex web of cultures with no less than 12 official languages.

I lived in Northern Ireland for many years. It is a beautiful country with wonderful people, but it has a legacy of trouble and oppression.

One of the most divisive topics in Northern Ireland politics today is the issue of languages, with various parts of the community speaking English, Irish, and Ulster Scots.

There is ongoing disagreement over which official languages should be used and what that means for government and education.

In South Africa, they navigated similar difficulties and challenges of disenfranchisement to build society.

Nelson Mandela did not do this alone and did not create a climate of fear while he worked.

There are countless examples of rebel leaders who build support from across communities with a vision to overthrow the government, but who eventually become dictators with fearsome reputations and oppressive regimes.

Leaders who see themselves as strong, clear and ambitious hold these aspects above all else.

Many see these traits as assets and can cite examples from business and politics to support their view that they should be operating this way.

But few commentators would agree that it is as straightforward as they expect.

Ethics are essential in recognising when these traits have gone too far. Unethical behaviour is likely to indicate a problem, and ethics are not just bound to legal and illegal acts but also to the way that people are treated.

Perhaps Mandela was aware of this when he left prison and distanced himself from violence and terrorism after his release?

In George Orwell's novel 1984, he describes a dystopian world where a country is ruled by a powerful elite.

The story follows one man and his exploration of rebellion against this all-powerful Big Brother, who polices everything, even the thoughts of the population.

There is a moment in the book when the main character, Winston Smith, is questioned by fellow rebels about how far he would go to win freedom.

He is asked if he will blow up civilians with a bomb or throw acid into the faces of innocents. Winston Smith says he will.

Later, under questioning by the Thought Police, he is asked about this. He is accused of being worse than the government, which is acting to prevent terrorism like this and protect innocents from attack.

It was a stark illustration of the dilemma people face in bringing about change, the lengths they will go to, and the ethics they employ.

There are examples of leaders who inspired change without compromising their ethics and demonstrated the importance of connecting with others to do so.

Leaders who create a toxic culture of fear are focused on results and have lost sight of the balance.

Their objectives are clear and they are dedicated to achieving them. They do not see the importance of the people around them unless they are on the same mission.

They may even use phrases such as "you are either with us, or against us"

They are on a mission for change, unflinching and inflexible when it comes to defining what success looks like, and they only want people around them chasing the same dream.

Mistakes are judged to be damaging to the cause. People want to hear success and progress, not problems, and they do not want to be slowed down by issues.

The Driving Force

Leaders who create a climate of fear because of a fear of making mistakes may often feel frustrated by a lack of progress.

I read a book by Laurence Rees called The Nazi Mind. It is a combination of historical investigation and psychological analysis that explores the rise of the Nazis during the 1920's, 30's and 40's.

In the book Laurence Rees explores the character, behaviour and strategies of dozens of prominent Nazi leaders including Adolf Hitler, in an attempt to explain how and why such atrocities were committed.

One aspect that he discusses often in the book is the deliberately vague agenda for Nazism.

Adolf Hitler, it appears, created a plan for the Nazis that was set out in points, but was very much open for interpretation by others.

This deliberately vague approach to leadership created instability among the people surrounding Hitler.

They were unable to clearly articulate the needs and goals of their daily activities without checking with Hitler for clarity, and often, programmes conflicted with each other.

Hitler used it to create tensions in the leadership and ensure he became central to decisions, guidance and mediation.

But it also became a point of frustration and anger for Hitler. He held a vision for a future Germany, but he did not have clear stages and goals for progress towards this vision.

His lack of clarity led to a group of people trying to follow the vision but guessing. Hitler created a culture of fear where mistakes were punished by death, through a deliberately unclear system..

A leader who has a clear vision but who does not have a clear idea about the specifics required to achieve it could create a climate of fear.

There is likely to be space between their expectations of the time required to achieve certain milestones and the reality of the problems faced.

This could create frustration, anger, resentment and a sense that the people around the leader are incompetent.

Have you ever had a manager who tells you to bring them "answers, not problems!"?

This could illustrate a leader who is unclear about what is required and instead relies on the group to do the thinking on their behalf.

They are challenging the team to find solutions to problems that they have not fully considered, which opens the possibility that they will blame others for finding problems where they believed none existed.

Revisiting the example of Martin Winterkorn from Volkswagen, we can see this theory in action.

His vision of tripling sales in the US was based on a huge market opportunity. Diesel cars comprise only a small percentage of the overall market, and emissions regulations were the main issue.

The route to his vision seems clear: create a diesel engine that exceeds the emissions standards necessary for the US and unlock a huge market opportunity that is hard to access for competitors.

However, the stages in reaching this vision are complex and time-consuming.

His lack of patience and empathy drove engineers to solve the problem, but in an unethical manner.

Compare this with the vision of President John F. Kennedy of the United States of America, who challenged NASA to land on the moon at a time when the team had barely safely returned a man from space, and the comparison is stark.

Kennedy provided an ambitious timescale, the end of the decade. Still, he also trusted the team to map out the stages and invested significant resources to find solutions to problems that had never been faced before.

He understood that what he asked was complex and would require detailed plans and stages of evolution.

Working Towards the Vision

A leader with a clear vision who creates a climate of fear through rejection of mistakes and intolerance is ambitious and impatient. They are likely to want positive thinkers who work towards results. They want teams that pay attention to details, which they might lack. They want people to present options and alternatives.

They are unlikely to know what stages and milestones exist in pursuit of the vision, so it is down to the team to map these out, but in a way that can be read as a map of the future, not as a series of problems.

As progress is made and problems are encountered, these leaders want to hear options and alternatives rather than face stark problems.

It will require a united team that is prepared to work together to support the realisation of the vision.

This team will be the driving force behind the leader's vision, creating pathways, solutions, ideas, and momentum.

This type of leader thrives on positive energy, focus, and progress. Dissenting voices will be best valued within the team of reports, where anticipated problems are a chance to find answers before the leader is involved.

Where there are options, these can be discussed and debated with the leader, but they will likely require recommendations and preferences.

This type of manager doesn't want to see the work behind the calculations; they want to see the finished product.

Imagine a complex performance at the theatre.

As the audience, we know there were months of rehearsals, we understand mistakes were made, and we recognise that not everything goes to plan during a performance. However, we want to enjoy the final result, not the journey.

So it is with managers who do not tolerate mistakes.

They simply want to focus on the final performance and let others manage behind the scenes.

You can find answers and work with colleagues to deliver when you understand this.

MANAGERS WHO RESIST CHANGE

From the perspective of today, it is hard to see a world where Google are not dominant in the tech industry. But there was a time when they were newcomers on the tech scene and were small when compared to technology titans such as Yahoo.

In 1998, Terry Semel, the CEO of Yahoo, was approached by Sergey Brin and Larry Page, founders of Google, who offered to sell him the business for $1 million.

They met with him again in 2001, when the price had risen to $5 billion, but again he walked away from the deal, reportedly offering only $3 billion.

Terry Semel was a former executive from Warner Bros., and he saw the internet in a different way from Sergey Brin and Larry Page.

He looked through the experience of traditional media such as newspapers, magazines and TV.

In these worlds, brand names dominated, and revenue was driven through advertisers who paid for exposure on platforms.

The greater the number of viewers, the more advertisers would be charged to place adverts in front of them.

He envisioned an internet where the public would use sites such as Yahoo as their home page. They would log in to access email, read news articles, and consume content.

His strategy was to place Yahoo at the centre of content creation. His strategy was to attract consumers to Yahoo to read and consume content in the same way that they might pick up a favourite newspaper or magazine or tune into a favoured TV channel.

He did not see a need for a search function, where consumers would leave the Yahoo site to find other content on the web.

The whole concept of what search was for and how Google would play such a pivotal role was alien to him.

With hindsight, his failure to buy Google was a catastrophic mistake. Yahoo missed the search revolution and eventually outsourced search to Bing. They lost relevance in the market and in 2017 were sold to Verizon for a fraction of their previous value.

His belief that Yahoo should be a media company and not a technology company was anchored in his past experience and his area of expertise.

He wanted Yahoo to be the latest version of something that he was comfortable with.

His view of the internet, which was reasonable back in 1998, was that it was a collection of pages like a magazine. His ideas, like a magazine, were that people were going to visit their favourite pages and consume content there.

What he missed was that very quickly, the internet became a magazine with billions of pages covering every topic imaginable!

The solution for such a complex set of pages was an indexing system where topics could be found using keywords.

This system exists in printed books, and even TV channels have a guide to help people find the content they want to watch.

Terry Semel did not understand this at all, and did not understand the role of Google as an indexing site helping people find what they wanted on the internet.

His resistance to change and the inability of the people around him to explain it in a way that made it clear how valuable sites like Google would become caused a catastrophe for Yahoo.

He stuck with ideas he had formed over decades. He stayed with a view of the world that was comfortable for him, and as times changed, he became irrelevant.

This is a familiar set of circumstances for many people struggling with a manager who resists change.

The problem with change is that while it is constant, it happens slowly.

Like a seedling growing in a pot, it is hard to see the changes day by day, but over a period of time, the seedling has transformed from a tiny green shoot to a flowering plant.

Executives such as Terry Semel are rarely proven wrong in a moment of transformation, but through an evolution of increasing irrelevance.

The story of RIM that we discussed earlier in the book follows a similar pattern.

A highly successful business is slowly caught up and overtaken by changing market dynamics and competitor evolution to the point where it becomes obsolete.

However, there are always people within the organisation who see the changes happening and who warn their leadership about the impending threats.

Why do certain leaders resist the changes, not heed the warnings, and ultimately lead their teams to failure?

The answer to this is complex and a combination of circumstances and personal fears.

I spent much of my career working in the pharmaceutical industry. This is a world where intellectual property is king, and there are significant investments being made into the research and development of the next blockbuster products.

Change and evolution are the heart of the business, and it is common to hear CEO's from the sector speak about the enormous risks that their businesses take to discover and develop products.

The nature of drug discovery means that it takes up to a decade to discover and develop a new medicine and that it might cost hundreds of millions of dollars to bring each one to market.

Of every drug that comes to market, there are likely to be dozens that fail, some of them at the final stages, after significant costs have been incurred.

As such, the industry is very protective of intellectual property and values it highly.

In 2014, GSK made what I consider to be an important mistake in strategy.

They had developed a series of very interesting products to treat various types of cancer.

However, they were a company steeped in the history of large primary care products, the types of medicines that are used by millions of people each year and are prescribed by thousands of doctors.

Cancer drugs are different.

They are highly specialised and they treat a fraction of the volume of patients. They are also prescribed by specialists in centres of excellence.

The other difference is that they are usually much higher cost drugs per unit, delivering similar total revenue to large volume drugs, but from a much lower volume of sales.

In 2014, GSK made the decision to sell a series of its most promising cancer drugs to one of its major rivals, Novartis. In return for the deal, GSK purchased some vaccines and the portfolio of over-the-counter medicines from Novartis.

The strategy was to remain aligned with the key strengths of GSK. They would boost the strong existing vaccine portfolio, add a series of important brands to the GSK consumer health division and sell off brands where GSK was less comfortable.

It was a strategy that was anchored in the past.

The mistake was that the business landscape was changing.

Consumer medicines are much lower-profit products because of the investments required to sell and distribute them. The appetite for large-scale vaccination is waning due to negative publicity and the success of previous vaccine programmes in wiping out many preventable diseases.

People simply do not feel the need to get vaccinated today like they did in the past, and the vaccine opportunity is large in developing countries where revenues are much lower.

There are many more limited opportunities with vaccination in the richer developed markets than in the developing world, and that will affect total revenue.

The pharmaceutical industry's upsurge in business opportunities over the last decade in developed nations has been due to the launch of new cancer treatments.

Cancer is a feared disease in many countries, and there remains a large need for innovative and effective drugs to treat it and save lives.

GSK sold off its best assets, its crown jewels!

The failure of the strategy was underpinned by the onset of the COVID-19 pandemic in 2020.

GSK is one of the global leaders in vaccine development, yet it failed to develop and launch an effective vaccine for COVID-19 in time to sign up for huge government contracts that were won by Pfizer, AstraZeneca, and Moderna.

Even in an area that GSK felt was a strength, they were unable to deliver on their hopes.

They have since chosen to invest in cancer treatments, spending $270 million in 2024 to buy early development products and have agreed to a partnership with a Chinese business to boost its pipeline of cancer treatments.

They are desperate to catch up in a key market where they gave away a commercial advantage to remain steadfast in their view of past glories.

Fear of Change, Fear of Loss

Successful businesses around the world, large and small, struggle with leaders who have built a career, a reputation and a business working in certain ways that they want to retain.

I witnessed this myself in consulting roles. I saw organisations struggle to refresh and update products because of leadership intransigence.

They were unable to successfully launch new products into new markets because they were fixated on pricing models, sales strategies, and internal structures.

The key question to explore in the context of leaders who resist change is, what does change represent for them?

I have heard senior leaders reject change because they believe that to accept that products and services need to change implies that they didn't produce the perfect product in the first place.

They hold a fear that to accept that it needs to change is to accept that there were problems in the product, and that means that they made mistakes.

To admit mistakes is to admit weakness, something impossible.

When leaders build organisations and invest years developing products, they pour themselves into the company and the brands.

When these elements are forced to change, it becomes a personal loss. To change means accepting that times have moved on and that all the energy to create what exists today needs to be repeated to create the solutions for tomorrow.

Think about the implications of that.

Building a career and a business takes years of dedication, sacrifice and stress.

Once the business is successful and thriving, the leader sitting at the top of the organisation wants to enjoy the fruits of their labour, not start again.

It is like climbing a mountain, sitting at the top, sweating after the tough climb, trying to enjoy the sunrise, only to be faced with the reality that you are not at the top.

If you add to that mix the fact that the skills that were used to drag the leader to the top of the business are no longer relevant, it is no surprise that leaders resist change and argue to defend the past.

If Terry Semel accepted that the internet was not just like a magazine or a TV channel, he would have to reinvent himself as a titan of technology, not a media mogul.

He is quoted as saying that Yahoo was a media company and not a technology company.

Their downfall was not embracing the world of technology.

GSK were a primary care and vaccines business. Developing and launching drugs for cancer requires a different set of skills and structures and would demand significant internal change.

It is much more comfortable to stay with an existing model that is doing OK than to risk failure when developing new strategies and new markets.

It is this argument that I witnessed in my own career.

A business doing incredibly well, growing successfully, was faced with the opportunity of exploring new product segments, with lower value, but higher volume clients.

They were debating the need to refresh and renew highly popular products, risking creating some dissatisfaction from existing clients, with the hope of offering something equally powerful in the future.

All this risk, uncertainty and change was debated in the context of leaders who wanted to enjoy the fruits of labour and to be reassured that their ideas remained as powerful and important as the day they were launched.

Leaders who resist change are likely to be fearful of failure, concerned about losing current success and protective of their ego.

It is no surprise that changes of leadership are often associated with a change in direction. Not only do the new leaders want to make their mark on the business, but they are unhindered by the past and able to make changes without personal risk.

Influencing managers who are resistant to change requires us to try to protect them from the changes they fear.

I wonder if explaining to Terry Semel that Google acted as an indexing site, the same way as in a book or a TV channel guide, might have helped him to see the importance as the internet exploded with pages?

Strategies that fail with this group are ones that try to highlight the differences between what exists now and what needs to exist in the future.

This comparison serves to highlight the breadth of the gap, the effort required to change and the lack of relevance of the past.

The internet today is much more of a media consumption tool than anything else. We share and watch videos, download books, read news articles and listen to music.

Yahoo, as a site, could have been similar to Netflix if it had incorporated search functions. Google, through YouTube, dominates content creation and sharing, and is perhaps the company that Yahoo could have been.

Change is much easier from a position of experience and with the resources of people, time and money that are available when businesses are already successful.

The lessons of the past are critical, and managers who are resistant to change are the best placed to lead change. Positioning them as the experts, tapping into their knowledge and ensuring that there are steps to protect the business from risk are the keys to unlocking a brave new future.

THE PROBLEM WITH DIFFICULT MANAGERS

By definition, our managers have power, and it is that power that can distort ways of working and behaving.

I read in Vulture Capitalism by Grace Blakeley that the contract of employment supersedes other laws, and by signing this contract, we agree to terms that we would not consider outside of work.

For example, if someone in the street came along and took money from your bag, you would call the police, and it would be a criminal matter.

In the work environment, theft is a serious offence and would likely result in someone losing their job, but not necessarily, and it is unlikely that there would be criminal proceedings.

In essence, the criminal act is overwritten by an employment contract, leaving the employer able to deal with the issue.

This is at the heart of difficulties when organisations fail to be held accountable for actions such as fraud.

Willingly misleading someone into paying money is a crime, but at a corporate level, these behaviours often go unpunished by criminal law.

The same is true for executives' behaviour towards women.

Many stories have come to light that illustrate the differences in how behaviour towards women at work has been treated compared to how the same behaviour in public would be treated.

This power dynamic becomes a key issue in the concerns over difficult managers.

Managers are often considered to be working with protection from the company and with the power to make decisions that could be judged to be unfair and unreasonable outside the work environment, but they are somehow protected by the business.

There is a fear that managers can act to end or damage careers and therefore have power over staff.

Difficult managers are tolerated by many because of a fear of speaking up and the consequences of doing so.

What this section has discussed, however, is not that managers are difficult as part of a power game, but that many of them are trying to deliver goals and objectives.

The difficulties arise because of the way they act and our perception of their behaviour.

Optimal long-term business performance is a balance of results and relationships. Unfortunately, we focus on the relationships more than the results because of leaders' and managers' perceived power.

Our fear of consequences after upsetting our manager discourages us from addressing issues proactively, and in essence, we suffer from an imbalance.

We need to overcome our fear of immediate repercussions and have a conversation with the goal of addressing issues and building trust.

In each of the cases we have discussed, managers do not act to exert power and control; they serve personal interests in the way they feel is best.

We need to accept that managers do not have the power we fear, and if they do, they will not use it simply because we want to have a conversation about how we can better work together.

If the intention of a conversation to address manager behaviour is to raise questions about the ways of working anchored in a desire to deliver results for them, then it is hard for them to dismiss discussions outright.

It is only when we are seeking to do less, or can be perceived as wanting to do less, that managers may react defensively.

Framing matters.

When asking for more flexibility, the interpretation from a manager might be that flexibility means you are doing less.

If you frame the conversation in a way that addresses their fears, depending on their personal goals and style, then you are minimising risks.

In the examples we have discussed in this chapter, the managers were keen to get things right, focus on the task and ensure that they were not embarrassed by being found not to have full oversight.

The way they operated was incompatible with certain expectations of behaviour, but it is hard to argue with the intention.

As such, dealing with difficult managers starts with understanding that you share the same ultimate objective - to deliver results.

The gap is in the level of trust they have in you to perform as they expect.

By exploring their fears, it is possible to unlock ways to work together and earn the trust you need to feel empowered, feel safe to make mistakes and feel able to build some flexibility into your schedule.

Managers are focused on success; they want teams around them who are skilled, confident and enthusiastic. They also need to know that they can trust you.

When you understand they are afraid of failure, that they have worries and that they are trying to defend their status, you can test strategies to build trust in non-threatening ways.

SECTION 04:
DIFFICULT CUSTOMERS

SALES IS EVERYWHERE AND FOR EVERYONE

When I talk about difficult customers, I frequently get a response from people saying that they don't have customers because they are not in sales, but that is not true. Sales is everywhere and for everyone, regardless of your function and level in the business. It goes beyond work, too. In our personal lives, we sell and influence others all the time!

A few months after John Pendlebury told me that my career as a professional rugby league player for Wigan was over, I found myself sitting in the Gerrard Arms in St Helens nursing a pint of Greenall's beer and thinking about the future.

The Gerrard Arms was a 15-minute walk from where I grew up and was a place where I spent many happy evenings with friends. It was a traditional English pub, with a crown-green bowling green at the back, a bar, and a lounge area. They didn't serve food, just beers and spirits, and it was a destination for locals to come, chat, laugh, and share packets of crisps.

After I turned 18, my closest friends and I would walk to the pub, share several rounds of beer, and then go to the closest fish and chip shop to buy food for the walk home.

I spent New Year's Eve there with my cousin, and another cousin worked behind the bar. It was also the place where my uncle bought me my first legal beer in a pub!

It was an important place and naturally a refuge I sought as I considered a new plan for the next ten years of my life.

I remember sitting in the lounge and looking at the people around me, trying to work out what to do about the future.

I suddenly had a realisation!

Sales are everything.

I looked around the room and saw that someone had sold everything: the furniture, the drinks behind the bar, and the snacks.

It went further. I had friends who worked in the building trade and others who worked as personal trainers. They were all selling. They needed to find new clients and close deals.

Over the years, I have understood that humans love to buy things. Whenever I travel to new cities, I always focus on markets and local traders. Restaurants, cafes and bars need to attract customers, and our major holidays are all anchored around the need to shop, gift and organise events.

This universal truth, that we love to buy, inspired me to realise that if I could sell, I would always be able to find work and make money, because there are always things to sell.

I went home and started to research sales jobs, only to discover a cousin who already worked in the medical technology industry in sales. She was instrumental in guiding me towards a role in the pharmaceutical industry.

She told me to buy "Great Answers to Tough Interview Questions" and prepare for interviews.

I already had science qualifications, and with some research and preparation, I felt able to secure my first proper job in sales.

Several months later, I joined an initial training course for Bristol-Myers Squibb as a contract salesperson, along with a team of others!

That was the start of the second phase of my career in pharmaceutical sales, and I loved it.

Over the years, I have been part of teams, projects, and groups from many different companies, industries, and functions, and I have become ever more convinced that everyone needs to sell and that it is a fundamental life skill.

An example of how I explain this to people I am working with is to compare two scenarios.

I ask them to imagine trying to persuade colleagues to make a decision and to try to influence that decision in their preferred way.

How might you approach that conversation? What information would you gather and share, and what arguments would you use?

Often, the response is a rather formal reaction, using a slide presentation and evidence to support arguments.

You might summarise it as a professional and polished set of arguments.

I then ask a second question: How would you persuade some friends to attend an event at your favourite restaurant?

This answer is revealing and much more attuned to the types of influence strategies that we fail to fully embrace in a professional environment.

They describe how they might speak with passion and enthusiasm. They explain the quality of the food and the personal service, and they appeal to their friendships, creating leverage through favours. Crucially, they rely on trust as a key strategy.

They understand that we can be influenced by people whom we trust, and we make decisions through emotions. These factors are most commonly used to influence our friends.

There are no slide decks, few pieces of data and more emotions.

This contrast illustrates some critical points about the importance of sales.

We are often natural salespeople; for some reason, we do not follow our instincts when trying to sell and influence at work.

The second point is that sales is not just about buyers and sellers.

Sales involves influencing others to make choices based on our recommendations, and that occurs every day with colleagues, managers, team members, and, of course, customers.

We need a certain level of trust to influence other people. When we have high levels of trust, it is easier to influence people, and that trust is earned over time.

Trust is not black and white, on or off. It might exist in very small amounts; indeed, there are times when it is barely there at all. We have just enough to start a conversation, and we immediately sense if it can grow enough to continue.

Consider meeting someone in the street and asking for directions.

At the moment you speak, there is very little trust, and even this situation is why many of us are uncomfortable speaking with strangers on the street, because we simply do not trust them!

But if you speak, you immediately try to understand if you trust this person enough to continue. Do they appear to be someone you trust enough to take advice from?

If not, you will walk away and find someone else to ask.

We will explore trust later and the elements that contribute to building trust commercially; however, it is a critical aspect and frequently difficult people at work, and indeed difficult customers are those with whom we struggle to build trust.

In this section, we will explore difficult customers. Difficult customers can be anyone you are trying to influence, and you do not have to be in sales to recognise the problems.

Customers can be other teams, departments, or functions that you partner with and want to influence, and difficult customers are those with whom this is not easy.

We are all able to influence and sell, especially with people we have great relationships with and trust.

Problems arise when we cannot connect on a personal level, making influence much harder, yet we are still expected to be able to work together productively.

A commercial edge comes to people who can work productively with people they naturally find difficult, and that is where opportunity lies.

UNREALISTIC EXPECTATIONS & DEMANDING SPECIAL TREATMENT

I was on holiday at Butlin's in Bognor Regis when I first came across the movie The Devil Wears Prada. My son was a few months old, and with two small children to entertain, it was the perfect place—full of entertainers, events, and activities.

There was also a cinema on site, and one evening, we decided to go and watch a movie, leaving the children with a babysitter.

I pride myself on being an easygoing person. I am flexible and understanding, so I rarely raise complaints as a customer. I start with positive intent, anticipating that people serving me in a restaurant or hotel are trying to do a good job. As long as the service is OK, I tolerate small issues.

When I saw The Devil Wears Prada, I was amazed at Miranda Priestly's attitude and treatment of people. Her standards were exacting and unforgiving.

There is a scene where Andrea arrives at her desk after running some errands for Miranda, to be greeted by a colleague desperate to run to the bathroom. She is afraid to leave the desk, even for a moment, to go to the toilet for fear of how Miranda will react.

Miranda set impossible standards for service on everything she did and for those around her. She always anticipated and expected perfection from everyone, and everyone who worked with her, served her or connected with her was expected to be perfect and faultless.

Fantasy?

Not exactly. The character of Miranda Priestly is based on Anna Wintour, the editor of Vogue Magazine, who is credited with transforming the magazine into a formidable fashion magazine recognised around the world.

She has high standards of delivery and expects the best from everyone. She is unflinching and unforgiving in her treatment of those around her.

There is a documentary called The September Edition that follows Anna Wintour through the development of the September 2007 issue of Vogue, the magazine's largest issue to date.

The documentary tracks how she was obsessed with every magazine detail, from the choice of models to the layout of each page.

She insisted on perfection and even demanded changes at the last minute. This created a high-stress environment among the people around her who were trying to satisfy her needs. Still, her perfectionism resulted in a groundbreaking issue that reset industry standards.

When I joined The Gap Partnership in 2014, I encountered a culture of exacting standards and excellence, where, as a business, we expected high standards from partners we worked with.

The business uses a wide range of hotels and conference centres around the world, within which the team delivers workshops for clients.

A culture of excellence in delivery was paramount in how we worked for clients, and those standards also applied to venues.

When we arrived at venues as consultants, we had procedures to follow to ensure the week's event ran smoothly.

Our capabilities as delivery consultants were partly assessed by the way we handled conference venues. The goal was to ensure that every client around the world received the same high standard of experience.

The team that managed quality in the business had very clear procedures and expectations for how the delivery team operated, and they were unrelenting in their pursuit of excellence.

When I joined the team, I found it inspiring and comforting.

It was an unapologetic focus on performance that many organisations can learn from. It was comforting for me because I wanted to ensure that I was doing the best job I could, and the standards set by the business provided me with justification to focus on the small elements without feeling guilty.

I remember arriving at a venue in Switzerland, a little late due to travel delays and marching into a meeting room.

My natural instinct to be accommodating and flexible, especially when under pressure, was put aside as I demanded that the room be laid out according to the specifications that were sent in advance.

I dealt with the restaurant team in a similar way to ensure that dinner was served promptly and supported our tight evening agenda.

My focus was on the client, who had invested significant resources in the event, and on making sure that the venue, for whom we paid handsomely, was delivering to the expected standards.

I don't know what the staff of this rather small and secluded family-run hotel thought about me marching about in my suit.

They were usually populated by tourists who used the hotel as a base for hiking and exploring the beautiful mountains surrounding the venue. The small pine wood tables and red and white checked tablecloths seemed somehow out of place in my corporate event, but my focus was on the workshop experience, not a holiday escape.

I learned much from my experiences working to the team's standards and implementing a level of excellence from the businesses we worked with. I also saw what happens when conflict arises.

One afternoon, we were in the office practising delivering exercises and case studies. By then, I had been in the business for several years and was highly respected for the quality of my workshop delivery, my knowledge, and my client relationships.

As was common during the afternoon, some debate arose about the optimal way to deliver the key messages and ensure participants learned the key points.

I disagreed with one of the key members of the quality team about how we teach the changing concept of opening extreme as relationships change during one of the cases.

This is a key aspect of how the team evolves learning during workshops, and the organisation sees it as a key turning point in client understanding.

I explained my perspective, and my colleague saw it differently. He wanted it explained exactly as it is written in the documentation.

Soon, a heated exchange ensued. We were both passionately focused on excellence, but could not agree on the best way to deliver it.

Neither of us backed down, fearing an overly tense argument, I excused myself and returned to my desk.

A few minutes later, my colleague came in and we found a way to agree.

It was a key moment for me to understand my growth as an expert who could debate details with such high-calibre leaders. Still, it is also a warning about the level of conflict that can arise when there are high standards and expectations.

Over the years, many clients have struggled with customers who want to be treated as special and feel that they need to have higher standards than others, which creates tension.

Small but Wants to be Big

I was engaged by a client who was changing terms with Amazon, and they wanted my support to help plan and execute the negotiations.

I was already supporting other parts of the business with price increases, and this element involved dealing with Amazon as a difficult customer.

There are many reasons why Amazon might be considered a difficult customer. Their business model is very different from traditional business-to-business relationships in retail; their ways of negotiating are different, and even their language is different.

In this case, Amazon was going to be a challenge because the company needed to change commercial terms in the UK to align more closely with European colleagues. This meant the terms would be less valuable for Amazon, and they didn't want to engage in the Amazon strategy of shifting to centralised purchases.

There was also time pressure; prices needed to be changed quickly to unlock value for the UK business and reduce risk across the wider European business.

For many organisations, Amazon is and continues to be a very important sales channel. Amazon data shows that consumers often use the Amazon website to search for and buy products in one place. Amazon is a one-stop shop for purchase, unlike other channels where consumers often search for information and then purchase elsewhere.

In many industries, this data makes Amazon powerful. They are stealing consumers from other channels and driving down prices, making large brands rethink their strategies for both digital and physical sales.

Amazon argues that it is democratising sales, reducing the power and influence of large brands, and putting consumers in charge through easy access, service levels, and low prices.

My client was in a different situation. It is a healthcare business that sells various personal care products over the counter.

Despite Amazon's dominance in categories such as electronics, it has had much less impact on healthcare. In the UK at the time, a very small percentage of company sales went through the Amazon channel. The biggest volume channels were supermarkets, high-street pharmacies such as Boots, and independent pharmacies via wholesaler customers.

My client was in a strong position with lots of easy-to-access alternatives, but Amazon's reaction made it obvious that they did not understand this.

When my clients presented the new terms to Amazon, they were very unhappy. They immediately responded with threats to stop selling certain products, and shortly after, to follow through and make a range of products unavailable on the website.

Over the next few weeks, the situation escalated, and leaders from my client business were called into meetings with Amazon executives to resolve the conflict.

It became clear that Amazon felt they should be treated very differently from what their share of sales suggested. They expected to be given the same terms and service levels as the largest customers my client worked with.

They demanded to be treated differently and used their position as a dominant retailer in many segments to pressure my client into making concessions.

One afternoon, we sat in a conference room in Birmingham discussing the situation with the negotiation team and decided that we needed to communicate assertively with Amazon about their real status. We felt that the overtures of partnership and joint working did not clearly articulate Amazon's lack of leverage.

We called a meeting between executives, during which the team presented the current status with Amazon. They outlined Amazon's role as a communication and advertising channel, which was valuable to the team. They also spoke of the availability of brands on the site through third parties, which consumers were satisfied with, and Amazon's relatively low market share across customer channels.

Amazon began to realise they did not have the power they expected, but demanded a plan to grow their relative share in the upcoming years.

This opportunity was enough for the teams to find a way to settle terms and plan for the future.

As Important as You Hope

A big part of our motivation in life is connected to status.

We seek to gain status from the people around us and want to protect the status that we have earned.

This status comes from achieving goals such as the exams we pass, the university we attend, and the job we have. It can be a function of knowledge, authority, or performance, and in many cases, it is hard-won through effort and dedication.

It can also come from our importance in the eyes of the suppliers who work with us.

If we are a large customer or see ourselves as somehow special, we demand special treatment in accordance with the status we have earned.

Miranda Priestly in The Devil Wears Prada and Anna Wintour, Editor of Vogue, earned their status through hard work, sacrifice and dedication. They used this power to further enhance their reputation and status through the pursuit of high standards, and these standards, in turn, drove further enhancement of their status.

Difficult customers who demand special treatment create problems for us because we must explore where they sit on the status scale.

Do they deserve to be treated as special, or are they demanding more than their real importance demands?

The difficulty is that there are costs associated with being treated as special. In the case of Amazon, they would be given commercial terms only available to larger customers, such as costs, revenue and profit.

Indeed, that is often a key purpose of customers who demand to be treated as special.

Yes, they want to feel special and important, they want their egos stroked and made to feel like they are central to your world, but they are also focused on value.

Numerous videos and posts are shared online by small businesses, who find themselves victims of social media influencers demanding to be treated as special.

I saw one where a social media influencer demanded free products for publicity for the small business.

The business owner was adamant that they were not going to give anything away for free, citing that the bank will not accept publicity as payment on debt, and neither will staff accept it as salary, so it has no value.

However, publicity has value, especially in a world of high competition, where celebrity endorsement can make a difference.

Anyone who has visited places such as Camden Food Market will understand this power.

One Sunday morning, I was there with my daughter when we encountered a queue around the block for a small ice cream parlour.

It was not the only one on site, so why was there such a long queue when the others were empty, I asked? The response was that the shop had become TikTok famous, and in fact, my daughter was excited to try it, before having second thoughts after fully appreciating the length of the queue!

Nevertheless, it is possible to secure discounts, better terms, better service and other benefits from being treated as special. As such, it is a key strategy employed by customers in many industry sectors to leverage terms.

Protecting Your Interests

If you want your customers and partners to feel special, you will find it hard to resist pressure from these customers to give them more value.

It is one of the key risks of a person who prioritises relationships over results and who lets the balance tip too far.

In some ways, you achieve your goal of making people the priority, but it backfires when they demand more of your attention.

Will Guidara is a restaurateur in New York who has made making customers feel special into an art form through his concept of unreasonable hospitality.

He focuses on finding small ways to exceed customer expectations, but to do so in ways that are hard to replicate for other restaurants and that are not flamboyant and costly.

For example, on one occasion, one of the team overheard a group of diners lamenting that they hadn't had the chance to sample New York's famous $2 street hot dogs on their trip.

In response, the team served the table these street treats and delighted their guests with a moment of magic.

He employs a Dream Weaver who is responsible for discovering and creating these magical moments. The weaver uses a unique combination of information about guest needs and empowerment to deliver magical moments.

The key for this type of experience when dealing with difficult customers is to ensure that they feel special and their ego is satisfied without undue costs.

Amazon didn't get improved commercial terms; in fact, they became worse. But they did get access to leadership and a three-year shared plan to build their status and importance in the business.

The goal is to make people feel special, but also retain a focus on results.

This requires courage to be open and direct about the true level of dependency that exists with that customer.

If they are indeed special, then try to find less costly ways to service them. If they are not special but demand to be treated as such, then you have a choice.

Use the power and leverage you have to say no, or to find low-cost opportunities to differentiate yourself.

Customer experience of buying is a huge factor in repeat business and loyalty. Therefore, ensuring you provide a great experience could be a powerful asset if you respect your need to deliver results and commercial value.

CONSTANTLY DEMANDING LOWER PRICES

Pricing is one of the most difficult factors to navigate in sales. So much of the buying and selling experience, so much of the work, the research, and the discussions, leads to an agreement over pricing. This is especially the case in business-to-business transactions, where the decision to purchase a product or service can hinge on the price.

It becomes such a critical moment in the sales process that many people try to delay it as long as possible and find ways to avoid it altogether.

The reason is that any final decision to cancel an order based on pricing could have such significant effects that people feel more comfortable avoiding it than facing it head-on.

There are also so many beliefs about the process of buying and selling that judgment can be easily clouded. There is no right way to discuss price; there are ways that might be more effective in a given situation, but people are so different that on another day, with another person, it will work perfectly.

I have a mantra that I repeat frequently with clients regarding price.

I explained to them that they have exactly the same objective as the buyers. You are both trying to agree on the best price possible; the only point of difference is what that price is.

There is comfort here because, at times, it can feel like there is a gulf between buyers and sellers when it comes to price.

Some buyers have turned pricing negotiations into an art form and into an impenetrable fortress where sellers enter at their own risk.

In 2021, during the COVID-19 pandemic, I ran an online event for some clients. The event was to support them with ideas and strategies for increasing prices during a time of immense pressure on stock, supply, and operating costs.

Afterwards, I was approached by one of the attendees at the event to discuss some specific advice and support for them and their team.

They were embarking on a price increase programme with their customers.

The pandemic, the pressures on their supply chain, the pressure of the market and other factors had forced them to act.

For the first time in 20 years, they were going to raise the prices of their products.

Nobody in the organisation at the time had experienced implementing a price increase before at that company, and they were understandably nervous about what might happen.

They manufactured products in the UK, and the need to increase prices was driven by the necessity to support wages and costs to continue this approach.

The challenge that they faced was interesting.

Supermarkets, their main volume customers, had a lot of power in the market. These supermarkets gained power through the relative volumes that they purchased, creating a strong dependency on them for revenue.

They were also highly aggressive about pricing.

Their policy was never to accept price increases from suppliers, and they created various barriers and processes that acted as defensive barriers to reduce the likelihood of suppliers attempting to increase prices.

Some of these barriers included buyers with fearsome reputations for being assertive, challenging and even aggressive in their manner when dealing with suppliers asking for price increases.

The supermarkets argued that they are protecting customers' interests by maintaining and even reducing the prices that they need to pay.

They defended consumer prices, they said, to stop multi-national suppliers from exploiting them.

The reality is that supermarkets themselves were fighting for market share in a competitive marketplace, and price was a key lever for them to use to attract shoppers.

The interesting challenge that the supplier had was that their products were fully made in the UK. This fact was something that they were very proud of, and it was something that consumers also liked.

Their consumer research demonstrated that customers were proud to support UK-based businesses and were prepared to pay more to do so.

Here was a source of conflict, a supermarket defending consumers, they claim want low prices, versus a company that claims that consumers will pay more for UK products.

The key question is, what is the truth? Do consumers pay more for products made at home?

Fair trade policies' success in encouraging price support for producers in the global south for products such as coffee suggests that they might.

This was something that my client was keen to leverage.

Exploring the market dynamics in the category further complicated the situation. They were not the only supplier in the category, and some of the competitors were large multinational companies.

They had the power to force through price increases and had done so in recent times. The shelf price of my client's products was not much lower than these alternatives and was a source of good margin for the supermarket, which was happy to retain the same price from the supplier, but increase the price to the consumer in line with other brands.

It is within this framework that we can see the complexity of the issue of pricing and customers who constantly demand lower prices.

It is a chain that is fueled at every stage by the needs of business and profits.

Manufacturers seek the lowest prices possible from their suppliers to support their business because they know that they will be required to offer low prices to customers. These customers are fighting in a market with others where prices are a key lever to attract consumers who are seeking low prices.

In the middle are suppliers who do not have the scale and resources to either structure their business to be the cheapest in the market or have the power to force customers to pay more.

We become caught in a trap fuelled by fairness.

The Fairness Trap

Humans have built enormous cities and cultures because of fairness and cooperation.

In his book Humankind, Rutger Bregman describes how cooperation plays a central role in why and how humans have come to dominate the planet like no other animal.

Language, writing, and communication have all played crucial roles in how we share information, passing knowledge to others and across generations, giving each future generation an advantage.

The next generation does not need to invent a way to build houses because the instructions have been passed down through time and can be evolved, improved, and refined.

Today, when I need to know how to perform a specific task, such as learning how to use my smartwatch or repairing damaged taps in the bathroom, I can open YouTube and find someone willing to teach me in a video.

We proactively share information and learning to provide others with opportunities and advantages that constantly enhance the whole human race.

This attitude is what Rutger Bregman explores in his book, challenging the assertion that we are selfish and underneath a veneer of cooperation, we are all animals, willing to steal and kill for what we want.

His research, including exploration of bombing during the Second World War, natural disasters and war itself, disproves this assertion and supports kindness as a universal instinct that must be overcome to release selfish and murderous behaviours.

Pricing becomes a crucial moment in time where our instincts to cooperate are tested.

We have natural instincts to act fairly and reasonably. These instincts are underpinned by cultural lessons and peer pressure that engrain a need to be fair to others.

We naturally fear being accused of being unfair, and as such, when we propose a price for goods and services, we are apprehensive of such accusations from our customers.

This is further enhanced when salespeople are focused on relationships with customers and desire to be liked by them.

Pricing discussions often represent a very small amount of time in the overall sales and customer relationship, with much more effort placed on trust building, understanding, and service delivery.

As a salesperson, if you spend 90% of your time trying to work closely with customers and your role relies on maintaining this closeness, then the fear of destroying this relationship for the sake of a small moment can be significant.

The fairness trap is characterised by a fear of being judged unfair by customers and, as such, offering them lower prices, when by doing so, you are acting unfairly to colleagues and suppliers who need to make sacrifices to fund your discounts.

Sales is a privilege.

It is one of the few functions that can generate revenue for the organisation, and with that power comes responsibility.

Salespeople who are irresponsible offer discounts to customers who accuse them of being unfair or unreasonable, and then colleagues or suppliers must accept lower wages or stagnant terms because they lack funds.

Difficult customers who constantly demand lower prices often tap into the fear of rejection and create a fear of loss in the minds of salespeople, creating pressure to conform.

The team I worked with in 2021 operated under this shadow for years.

In the early days, every time they approached customers requesting price increases, they were met with threats to stop buying products and to switch to an alternative.

The reaction they received was clear rejection and accusations of unfairness against consumers.

Together, these threats and fears mounted up to become barriers that my client stopped trying to overcome.

Only the real pressures caused by economic transformation forced them to confront these barriers and seek advice on how to overcome them.

Creating the Other

If we are all built to cooperate and act fairly and reasonably, then how can certain difficult buyers constantly demand lower prices and act apparently against this instinct?

Part of the answer comes from how we react to strangers.

When we meet someone new, part of our system is dedicated to assessing whether they are a threat.

I imagine it a little like a sentry on duty at a gate. As a stranger approaches the gate, the sentry demands to know if they are friend or foe, hoping to receive an honest answer from a possible enemy.

Our brain gathers as much information as possible in those first few seconds to protect us from an unseen threat. It will use information from body language, appearance, language, tone, and context to inform us if this new person is one of us or one of them.

This question is important because we are finely tuned to feel safe with someone like us, and unsafe with people we deem to be the other.

This is a contributing factor to explaining why certain connection strategies are effective in encouraging us to like other people when we first meet.

In The Psychology of Persuasion, Robert Cialdini explores a number of influence strategies, such as 'liking,' that affect how we react to new people.

In liking, we connect to something that we share in common with another person, and it gives us reassurance. Robert Cialdini explains that it can be something as simple as a shared name or shared town of birth, and shared connections with others are a highly potent factor.

This information suggests that the person we are meeting is like us and, as such, no threat.

Our nature and binary approach to this choice of them or us means that we are very susceptible to strategies that create a sense of the other.

As a young sales representative, I heard a Sales Director present such an argument, which had potent effects on my attitude.

It was around the time that The Lord of the Rings: The Two Towers was in cinemas. The story follows Bilbo's ongoing quest to destroy a ring of power in a fantasy world filled with elves, dwarves, dragons, wizards, and magic.

Their enemy is a wizard and an army of Orcs. These orcs are monstrous creatures, powerfully built, aggressive, ugly, and scarred. They are filled with hate, know war, death, and killing, and are utterly relentless and merciless.

They are a formidable force and are produced in their thousands to wreak destruction across the land.

We were at a sales briefing meeting, and after a two-day event, our sales director took the stage to deliver the final call to action.

He wanted to inspire and motivate us to new heights, and he did so by invoking the potent power of the other.

He talked about our main competition and their sales team. He painted a vivid picture for the audience, describing them as orcs pouring out onto the plains of Middle-earth.

It demonised them and acted as a glue, uniting our team against a common and dangerous foe.

We had one mission: to defeat them.

The truth is that this group of people were in fact exactly the same as us. They were a mixed group of professionals working with customers to sell their products and to develop their careers.

Both products were excellent choices for customers and delivered different but valuable functions.

They were not Orcs, they were not evil, and they were not out to destroy us. They were good, honest people working hard to do a good job.

Using the other is a simple and powerful tool often used in business to create division and justify decisions.

When there is a 'them versus us' situation and arguments can be made that present us as honourable, it is easy to make demands and push for ever-lower prices.

Buyers who believe that they are justified in demanding lower prices because they are defending the value of their business, their customers and their colleagues will have no problem challenging terms presented by suppliers.

Doing the Job

There is something else at play when buyers constantly demand lower prices.

They are doing their job,

Salespeople have two key levers that they can use to deliver value to their business. They can sell products at higher prices and, as such, increase revenue; they can also sell a greater volume of products at the same price and increase revenue.

The dream is to sell greater volumes at higher prices!

The role of sales in delivering revenue to businesses explains why business leaders usually consider them an investment.

A sales force is assessed less by its cost and more by the revenue it generates for the business.

Buying is different.

Buyers are a cost for any organisation. Their wages and costs are expenditures that are only increased by their activities, which involve spending company money to buy resources.

A decision to recruit a buying team is often taken carefully, with very limited numbers, because of the costs associated with them.

Salespeople have the luxury of being able to focus on the lever of volume to justify their existence and avoid too much focus on pricing.

They can find ways to sell more volume when they need to achieve their targets.

Buyers who are trying to carve out a reputation for excellence and be highly respected by achieving targets need to drive down acquisition costs.

During workshops, I often ask clients how they want others to talk about them in end-of-year reviews.

They respond with words such as high-performer, respected, talented, leader, delivers results, achiever, team player, and future potential.

Because of my experience, I spend most of my time working with sales teams, but when I talk with buyers and procurement professionals, their answers are the same.

They, too, want to be known for excellence, and their careers and security depend on them delivering for the business.

That requires them to be conscious of costs and the price paid.

Buyers are constantly demanding lower prices to serve their internal needs to be successful and secure.

They work hard to represent their business, a business that they feel loyal to protect and serve. They might feel that they are working to deliver results to protect their colleagues and customers from external factors seeking to exploit them and that they are doing the best job they can to achieve their personal goals.

Own the Moral High Ground

Fairness plays such a central role in pricing and the conflict between buyers and sellers that it also needs to be part of the solution.

Trust is essential for sales. We will only buy from people we trust because we fear being taken advantage of by others.

As salespeople, much of our energy goes into building and nurturing trust with customers, hence the need to focus on the balance between results and relationships.

The same is not entirely true of buying. There is less onus on them to build trust with suppliers, perhaps due to the effort that suppliers put into building it, but also because they gain strength from the ability to quickly switch suppliers.

Suppliers want to create personal and professional dependency from buyers to create stickiness.

Buyers want to reduce this because when they can switch easily, they retain the power to drive down prices, something we have seen is their only major lever.

Buyers' reliance on strong relationships as a lever of value has little or no value except to ensure they have supply, which is often controlled through contracting.

However, they do use the threat of cancelled relationships and the hope of building a better relationship as levers.

Buyers will offer partnerships, preferred status and other elements as tools to encourage better prices. They will also cancel these privileges and meetings with senior people as tactics to create pressure on suppliers because they understand the value they hold.

This means that it is harder for sellers to find ways to unite with buyers towards a shared goal within the relationship.

But creating a shared focus is an important step in dissolving any potential barrier between 'them and us.'

When we see the individual behind the group identity, we are less likely to hold the same views as previously.

Buyers who constantly demand lower prices do so partly to justify a bigger mission to support their business or their customers. Here is the opportunity to form an alliance and break the barriers.

Finding ways to join this shared mission to help their business or to deliver for consumers makes a huge difference in the ability to resist pressure to cut prices.

My client laid out a dual strategy for the buying teams designed to shift their thinking. They successfully argued that they had not asked for increased prices for many years and, as such, had actively supported their business with a margin.

They also argued that competitors who had raised prices were a common enemy and were damaging the business. A price increase for them and a shift of volume from competition would benefit both parties, they argued.

The supermarket questioned how this additional volume would be delivered in such a price-sensitive and brand-led market.

The answer was to leverage consumer preference for locally produced products, the creation of local jobs, and the ethical behaviour of a producer during a global crisis.

It was a strategy that worked effectively and saw not only price, but volume increases for my client.

Account managers often become susceptible to the 'them and us' strategy when they spend too much time with customers and become sympathetic to their cause.

Their success is closely tied to that of a small group of customers, and it can become a problem.

Telling customers that they cannot have lower prices, facing threats of cancelled orders, and being accused of damaging relationships are huge fears that, over time, take a toll.

It becomes easier to fight for better prices for customers against your own organisation, and appear to switch allegiances.

To fight this, it is essential to retain the moral argument and be clear about what the business stands for.

This is why I focus so hard on the business's mission and the sales and commercial team's responsibility to their colleagues and suppliers.

Dealing with demanding, difficult customers who constantly seek lower prices requires determination, passion, courage, and a sense of moral virtue.

The promise of a bonus and a promotion is not enough.

MISLEADING INFORMATION, OMITTING INFORMATION & IGNORING OBJECTIONS

I read an article published online, an open letter to the NHS in the UK, from the CEO of a technology company.

In the letter, he described trying to do business with the NHS as 'a challenge of survival,' not one of pleasure.

He outlined the length of time it takes them to make procurement decisions, the frequency of pilot programmes that are eventually cancelled, the fear of innovation, and the glacial pace of adoption.

He describes the companies that are successful in this environment as those that survive long enough to finally win a contract.

He comments that the stated intentions to procure innovation and to establish a dynamic business environment are fabrications. The reality he describes is very different, slow, cautious and torturous.

Salespeople have a reputation for misleading potential customers, and the stories of scammers that circulate are lodged in our minds.

We fear the salesperson who uses manipulative tactics, who misleads us and who perhaps is prepared to lie to us to close a sale.

But this open letter illustrates that it is not just unscrupulous sales-people who are misleading. Procurement teams also have the incentive to do the same.

The 1980s were a time of property liberation in the UK. Political changes dramatically increased property ownership, creating financial incentives to improve properties to deliver returns on investment. It was during the 1980s that the seeds of the growth of property development for the masses were sewn.

A key strategy for property improvement was replacing old, draughty, and cold windows with new double-glazed units. These units were designed to improve the look, economy, and value of houses and were a dramatic improvement on the old single-paned glass units of the past.

This environment gave rise to a plethora of companies selling and installing windows and doors, and without formal regulation, they started to build a formidable reputation.

They created a reputation as places where salespeople could earn significant money through commissions, but also where these incentives drove unethical practices from salespeople.

They became famous for pushy tactics, exaggerated claims and ignoring questions from customers.

The TV series White Gold aired in the UK by the BBC, followed by a sales team with a comedic eye on their tactics. During the series, we witness salesmen refusing to leave customers' homes, even late in the evening, until they have closed a sale.

We see how they cover up poor production quality and get customers to sign up for finance packages without fully explaining the details.

Sadly, these behaviours do not only exist in fantasy.

In the early 2000s, in the UK, if you went to buy a car or took out a personal loan to pay for home improvements, it was highly likely that you had Payment Protection Insurance included with the loan.

This simple idea was designed to reassure customers in the event that they were unable to repay loans. Customers would add an additional fee to their monthly repayments, and if, within the terms and conditions of the insurance, they were unable to make the payments, the insurance would kick in.

These were heady days for consumers before the global financial crisis of 2008, when easy credit and low interest rates were available.

This additional product was designed by banks and institutions to give assurance to borrowers and encourage them to take more loans.

The problem was that the product was a huge fraud, and companies were guilty of mis-selling payment protection insurance (PPI).

Lloyds Bank was one of the banks found to have been one of the most prolific offenders and was eventually forced to repay more than £18 billion to consumers for its actions.

Many customers were unaware that they had bought PPI when they took out loans.

It was automatically added to their monthly premiums, and they were expected to have read all the terms and conditions in detail and chosen to opt out if they believed that they did not need it.

It was also found that many customers who were paying for PPI, either with or without their knowledge, were, in fact, ineligible for its benefits in the event that they might make a claim.

Certain exclusions, such as those for people with existing medical conditions or the self-employed, were never clearly explained to customers, rendering them ineligible for payments.

Banks were guilty of offering staff incentives to sell PPI that encouraged unethical behaviour, such as telling customers that PPI was a mandatory requirement of the loan agreement.

They were also accused of inadequate training for staff and directing them to assure complainers that the process of selling PPI was legally compliant, and thus rejecting any claims of mis-selling.

The massive scale of the fraud became apparent in the mid-2000s after numerous complaints to the Citizens Advice Bureau and Financial Conduct Authority were investigated and upheld.

The scandal meant that banks set aside almost £50 billion to repay money and settle compensation claims. Regulations were put in place to protect consumers from this type of behaviour in the future.

Given the money, it is easy to understand the purpose of the behaviours we have seen here: unscrupulous salespeople pushing double glazing on to customers and crooked banks exploiting customers' fears.

In fact, these examples resulted in changes to regulations to protect consumer rights in the UK and to allow companies to take action against those who broke the rules.

Around the world, consumer rights have been developed in many markets to stop large organisations from exploiting customers, and there are constant debates between governments, political opponents, company lobbyists and consumer protection groups on the scope and power of these regulations.

Companies want a relaxation of rules to allow them more freedom to act without regulation, and consumer rights groups want to ensure that vulnerable people are protected.

However, aside from these high-profile cases, the use of misleading information by people at work, especially in business-to-business agreements, can be subtle but also powerful.

A key negotiation strategy and one of the factors that I identify as a key performance indicator for negotiation outcomes is the importance of framing and positioning.

This skill is the ability to set the agenda and the negotiation boundaries through the communicated messages.

It can be very simple to do and very effective when done well. For example, a client approached me on a call one afternoon.

They wanted to use the skill of opening with ambition in a negotiation, demanding terms that were much lower than they really needed, to create space for movement, a movement that would allow the other party to feel successful.

Opening with ambition is an important skill to demand a lot more, or a lot less than you require, knowing that you are going to offer concessions and provide the other party with a feeling of personal achievement.

The reason for their question was that the deal they were discussing was based on a renegotiation of a previous contract. The customer had set an expectation that the previous investment would be increased by at least 5%.

My client intended to offer 0% initially, but was worried that it was not a credible position given the demand for 'at least a 5% increase'.

His question gave me important insight. Through this statement, the customer had set the frame of the negotiation, and any proposals lower than 5% could be rejected outright as outside of the frame of the deal that was to be agreed.

I asked him, "If they had not made that suggestion, what would you propose?" His answer was to reduce investment because they had not seen the value that they had hoped for in the previous contract.

My response was to explain to him that this is the frame from which you must approach this negotiation and use it to position your proposal.

When you say, "We have not seen the performance of the contract that we hoped for, and while we intend to continue working together, we cannot invest as much as previously," you have created a new frame that makes a proposal of -3% investment seem credible.

In this scenario, maintaining the investment as it was previously would seem to be a possible outcome, enabling the customer to feel alright about it.

If the initial frame was a reduction in investment and instead, through their hard work, they achieve the same investment, that is a success, relatively speaking.

This example illustrates the power of positioning in negotiation and why the party that dominates the position usually achieves their goals in the ultimate deal.

However, it also illustrates the space between parties when they meet and how information becomes a tool to create pressure and leverage

Either party will selectively choose information to present that most strongly illustrates the case they are trying to prove. They are likely to ignore data that does not help them, and they will fail to fully answer questions and objections that open their arguments to scrutiny.

In certain industries, buyers who are faced with increased acquisition costs often demand a full breakdown of production costs. They want to see the costs of every element of production and distribution, and an explanation of why costs have increased so much.

Their goal is to find inconsistencies and create arguments that they can use to cancel or reduce the cost increase.

Experienced salespeople recognise this strategy from the buyers, and they avoid sharing information or making any explanations.

Information is power; the more that you have, the more power you can generate by using the information to help your arguments.

Negotiators talk of information asymmetry, where the party with the most information has more power.

The reality is that it is almost impossible to know how much the other party really knows until much later.

At a pricing negotiation, I was once faced with this dilemma.

Our goal was to increase the cost of a key brand that we were selling, and the customer objected strongly. They, as the largest customer in the market, demanded the lowest prices in the market.

We were confident that they were the customer with the best prices, even with the increase.

Then they presented us with a proposal: They would accept the new price, but if they could find any examples in the last three months where they were not the lowest prices in the market, then we would give them the stock over that period for 1p per unit.

We took a time out from the negotiation room and sat as a group to consider our options. We remained confident that they were the lowest-priced customer, but we were faced with the possibility that, among the thousands of customers, someone might, even for a week, have been given better terms. It could have been an error, but that would not matter, and we were concerned that our customer had somehow discovered this exception to use to unlock millions of pounds for his business.

Here was an asymmetry of information; did he know something we did not?

It was too large a risk to take, and instead we chose to make an alternative proposal.

Even today, I have no idea whether that was a bluff or if he did have some information; I will never know.

These stories illustrate the importance of information in delivering commercial results. When information is this important to business deals, customers are motivated to manage it carefully.

It is in their interests to choose information that supports their argument and to ignore data that does not.

They benefit from refusing to answer questions fully or to provide incomplete answers because by doing so, they protect their commercial interests.

Personal & Commercial Interests

In 2017, Charlie Javice founded a company that evolved into FRANK. It was a simple idea: her company would help students to complete the complex forms required to apply for financial aid.

Students are a key target audience of banks because the rate of switching from bank to bank is so low after accounts are opened, and JPMorgan Chase & Co. saw an opportunity to get access to this lucrative market segment.

In 2021, Charlie Javice expressed interest in selling the company and ultimately secured a deal with JPMorgan Chase & Co for $175 million, of which she was due to make $45 million.

However, the deal was not everything that it appeared to be. Charlie Javice conspired with others to inflate the real number of customers that she had from 400,000 to 2,000,000 in order to inflate the value of the company.

She was convicted of fraud in 2025 and could be sent to prison. After the fraud was discovered, JPMorgan Chase & Co. closed down the FRANK business entirely, and Charlie Javice could be liable for payments and fines as a result of the conviction.

There is an obvious financial incentive for Charlie Javice to commit fraud in this case, which is consistent with what we have seen previously, but what is also of note are the personal gains associated with the case.

There is a culture surrounding successful founders and entrepreneurs, especially in the tech sector. Before the case came to light, Charlie Javice was named in the Forbes 30 Under 30 list and was widely regarded as a talent in the industry.

Associated fame, status, recognition, and success, on top of financial gains, tempt people to become difficult in the way they manage, manipulate, and ignore information.

Emotional gains such as status, fame and becoming a thought leader are powerful for many people at work.

As we have seen, it can be difficult to uncover the truth when people have been misled by information. Many of the cases in this chapter came to light after a serious investigation.

The added layer that, at times, information is open to interpretation and therefore hard to prove as right or wrong, means the rewards for being manipulative can outweigh the risks of being caught.

People who exclude, ignore, or use misleading information to further their financial or personal gains might think they are helping themselves at no risk.

It is so important that many people are tempted to make small changes and exclusions to their personal gain.

Do you know someone who has changed details on their curriculum vitae when applying for a job, or who has failed to share all the risks of a project that they want to be approved by colleagues?

Indeed, this issue is one that many people can relate to at some level, which makes it easier to understand but also harder to protect against.

Avoid Being Misled

Buyer beware, or so says the warning to people buying second-hand products.

When I bought my first car, I was very excited. I had been paid a large signing bonus from Wigan, and I knew that I was going to buy my first car! I was going to be clever and buy something reliable, but also used, because I was going to drive a lot, and as a new driver, I was aware of the high insurance costs.

I looked through the papers, where used cars were advertised in the days before the internet, and I found a Ford Orion that looked great!

I went to the garage, test-drove the car, and fell in love. I put down my deposit and went home to gather my thoughts.

Later that day, I called a friend to tell him about the car. He suggested getting the AA to look at it. He said, "You know nothing about cars, and this is a lot of money to waste!" He was right.

I called the AA and paid for an engineer to look at the car.

A week later, I had the report in my hand, and I was disappointed.

They found a list of problems with the car, including accident damage repair in the rear, that would have left the car susceptible to damage in the future.

I called the garage and cancelled my order, and I was so disappointed.

Looking back, I find it strange that I felt so disappointed, because I should have felt relieved and proud.

I had just escaped from an expensive and embarrassing purchase. It was one of the smartest things I could have done.

Instead, a few weeks later, I bought a navy blue Vauxhall Astra that I loved!

When we make business decisions and listen to others deliver proposals, we should assume that they are painting the best picture and using information to their advantage.

This is true for salespeople seeking to close a sale. Still, it is also true for buyers who are trying to paint a certain picture to justify better terms, for colleagues who are trying to influence our choices for projects and budget and for managers who want our support.

There is much to gain from painting a positive picture or editing it in a way that helps us, but we should be cautious.

Be prepared to do research and find alternative sources of data and reports, where possible.

Make lists of questions that are important to understand and invest energy in mapping out your risks and worries.

The most important piece of advice is to persist in chasing answers.

People who are trying to manipulate will evade questions and make you feel guilty for asking and probing them.

They will use tactics to make you feel uncomfortable, such as time pressure and even threats, to force you to stop asking. These tactics should act as triggers to warn you to explore further and set your mind at rest.

In the end, you should explore the possible risks and decide if you are prepared to take them, but do so in your own time and using information gathered from reliable sources.

UNLOCKING THE SECRETS OF DIFFICULT CUSTOMERS

There is a myth about the so-called "Stockholm Syndrome" where it was believed that hostages in a siege started to empathise with their captors.

It is a myth because when revisiting the case, it was clear that the hostages in the case were not empathising with the captors, but were afraid of the actions of the authorities. They felt that the best way to survive was to stop a full-on assault from the authorities.

Their behaviour was misinterpreted, and for years, we have become accustomed to the idea that it is possible to connect with people who should be the enemy.

It is a phrase commonly used to describe people who shouldn't sympathise with the people they are with. Hostages should not be helping their captors, and when they did so, it was interpreted as betrayal.

The truth was that the hostages were serving themselves first. At certain points during the siege, they chose to support the hostage takers because it was in their interests to do so.

I use this example because that is the strategy of many difficult customers.

Our customers are serving their own interests, trying to secure optimal prices, favourable treatment, or to look good to their leadership.

Conflict arises because we are in the way.

We serve our own needs, goals, and business. We want to ensure we secure margin, close deals quickly, and avoid giving away too much value.

The easiest way for customers to get us to switch allegiance is to demonstrate to us that it is in our interests to do so.

We, as humans, constantly try to make our lives easier. Many of the inventions of the last 100 years are tools and devices that make performing regular tasks faster, easier or more convenient.

Human ingenuity has constantly chased the creation of tools that make life easier, and we apply the same principles to relationships with customers, as well as others at work.

Results are long-term objectives, perhaps a year away, maybe months away. We are not very good at thinking about the future.

Our inner emotional voice seeks immediate gratification. It is a powerful voice, and it is a loud voice. When it tells us that we deserve a glass of wine after such a hard day, it demands it now.

It does not consider the promise we made to ourselves to drink only on weekends to help us sleep better and wake feeling fresher.

Gratification needs to be now.

The idea of waiting to achieve business results that will arrive in several months' time is a very hard concept to accept, especially when faced with stress and discomfort right now.

A difficult customer, demanding better, makes us feel stressed because we naturally want to build a positive relationship with them.

Their dissatisfaction, when voiced, feels awful.

We fear rejection, we fear losing opportunities, and we fear judgment from colleagues and managers.

Those feelings, like the desire to drink wine, are powerful and immediate.

Our negative emotions are strong, and the difficult customer is offering us a way to make those negative feelings go away. They are offering us a way to serve our own interests.

By giving in to their demands, we make ourselves feel better, we escape stress, anxiety, and we can easily justify it by arguing that we are protecting our relationship with the customer and what we have agreed to is low cost anyway.

I see this scenario play out regularly with clients during events and as we are working through business challenges.

The feelings are real, the fears are real, and the justification of keeping a customer happy is real.

The problem is that it is not necessarily the right choice for the organisation and the long term. It is not necessarily the right decision for us.

Perhaps future you would be more grateful that you said no and stood your ground, so that they had more credibility with the customer and were in a stronger position to achieve personal milestones.

Difficult customers are using strategies that play on fears and emotions to pressure concessions.

If you understand what they are doing, they will not give you credit for helping them. On the contrary, they have learned what to say and do in order to gain your compliance, and they will do it again.

You need the courage to focus on your own personal goals long-term, not short-term escape from tension.

You need to recognise that they are manipulating you and ensure that you serve your own and your company's interests first.

A balance of results and relationships earns respect from customers. It enables you to draw boundaries and start the journey to building trust.

SECTION 05:
HOW TO SUCCEED

TRUST

Trust is central to all personal relationships, but for the purpose of the book, I will focus on commercial relationships.

Trust is not absolute, it is not binary; you do not either have trust, or you do not. There are degrees of trust, and even the first time you meet someone, there is at least some trust in existence.

How you behave in the first few seconds of a conversation impacts your trust levels with each other. You might do something that increases trust, or you might do something that damages trust, but you have somehow changed your level of trust, not created it.

Indeed, we often start with more trust than perhaps people deserve.

We make assumptions about people based upon the place we meet them, the context, the way they look, the way we are feeling at that moment and a host of other factors.

We usually give people the benefit of the doubt, choosing to offer some degree of trust until they have proven to us that we should either diminish or increase it.

It is often easier to work with someone new, with whom there is no history of trust, than with someone who has breached the trust we had built.

For this reason, changing the people in a customer relationship or negotiation when trust has broken down can be highly effective.

Even though the commercial situation is largely the same, perhaps a conflict over pricing or contract terms, a change in people can trigger progress because there is more trust, and people are prepared to offer more flexibility.

It is only with long-established conflicts between bodies, such as trade unions and managers, that changing people does not significantly change the dynamic. Even then, new faces are a welcome change that can trigger new discussions.

When we analyse the challenges of various difficult people, it can boil down to issues related to trust.

Exploring the trust relationship between you can highlight problems and suggest strategies for improving the situation.

Trust is strange because it is a mutual emotion. Both parties experience it, and both parties have their own interpretation, which is why some people appear difficult to you and others do not.

It is a strong possibility that you do not share as much trust with the people you find difficult, compared to the people you work well with, and that is the source of the problem, but is it also highly likely that they do not have high levels of trust in you?

Any imbalance of trust will create discomfort, misunderstanding and difficulties.

It is our responsibility to explore the trust we have and do not have with difficult people, to be honest about what the problems could be, and to take steps to adjust.

Difficult people never intend to be difficult because they are operating within their norms. If we have issues and we see commercial value in seeing past these issues, then it is down to us to be accountable for making change happen and adjusting our behaviour.

A commercial edge comes when you are prepared to make changes to succeed with people whom you previously saw as difficult. This is a new source of opportunity, and being accountable for implementing change, even if it is uncomfortable, will make a huge difference.

I have identified five elements that are a recipe for trusted relationships that balance results and relationships. These elements are not present in equal proportions and can vary from person to person. When a relationship is difficult, one of the likely causes is a low level of one of these elements, and the result can be a knock-on effect that influences other aspects.

Building trust requires investment in developing these ingredients, taking time to understand where problems exist, even if they are within the perception of the other person, and taking steps to change their belief.

Securing trust is the main route to finding the balance of results and relationships that we discussed earlier. It is rare that we will be in a commercial relationship with someone, have high levels of trust as defined by the five ingredients and not feel there is a balance of results and relationships.

The difficult people we encounter at work are usually so because one or more elements in either their or your perception are faulty.

THE FIVE ELEMENTS OF TRUST

In my experience, the five elements of trust are a deep understanding of goals and motives, the realisation of value for both sides, credibility and empowerment of the people involved, reliability of delivery and finally vulnerability and humility.

The absence of any of these aspects causes problems and is likely to be an issue with difficult people at work.

Let's explore each in turn to understand their relevance and how we can work to improve them in our commercial relationships.

Deep Understanding

The people we trust the most are also the people who know the most about us. They are the ones who know our secrets, our hopes and dreams and both our strengths and weaknesses.

When we meet someone new, we are usually careful about the types of information that we are prepared to share with them.

Information and understanding about us is layered, and the deeper the layer that is exposed, the more trust we need to have with the people we share it with. This is because the deeper the understanding we share, the more personal it becomes.

Our actions are the outermost layer. What we say and do is obvious to everyone around us. Our choices can be easily witnessed by anyone who shows an interest.

If I go for lunch, you can observe what choices I make. If I choose a vegetarian option at the counter, everyone can see that.

What is unclear is the reasoning behind my decision. Why did I choose a vegetarian meal on that day?

It is at this outermost layer that we can make grave mistakes with trust. We notice what people do and say, but we do not explore further to understand why. Instead, it is easy to make assumptions and guess, applying our own thinking and beliefs rather than asking them.

Assumptions and guesses can be wrong, and when they are, we immediately damage trust and leave people feeling like we do not know them or care about them.

For example, I could choose the vegetarian meal because I am concerned about animal welfare, and have made a choice to be a vegetarian.

If you assume that is the case, then you are going to assume other things about me that might be common for vegetarians.

But I could have chosen a vegetarian meal for reasons that have nothing to do with my feelings about animal welfare.

Perhaps I intend to cut down on my meat consumption because of concerns about carbon emissions from animals, to make healthier choices because of doctors' advice, because I have allergies to certain types of meat, religious beliefs or simply because on that day the vegetarian option was the most tempting menu choice.

Each of these reasons is distinct and may be connected to my different beliefs and feelings, but they are all accompanied by the same action.

When we want to increase our level of trust with someone, we need to explore their actions more deeply than simply observing them. We need to get into the next layers.

Underneath actions are attitudes. We have certain attitudes towards our actions. These attitudes stem from our beliefs, which are a combination of experiences and culture. At the heart of our decisions are feelings, where we are most guarded.

As we explore choices, we need to delve layer by layer, especially with people whom we see as difficult.

Sharing our innermost feelings and beliefs with others is a very personal experience, and we do so when we feel safe, because it is with someone we trust.

Therefore, we are unlikely to share feelings with someone difficult because there is low trust and low safety, but paradoxically, sharing more information will help build trust.

Reciprocity plays an important role here. By actively sharing a little more about ourselves, we can encourage others to share more about themselves.

It requires patience, curiosity, and the need to be genuinely interested in their responses.

If you sat with me for lunch and noticed that I chose the vegetarian option, how might you uncover more about why I did so?

Do not ask me, "Why did you choose the vegetarian option?"

Asking 'why' is both challenging and personal. It implies judgment, especially if delivered sharply, and can easily make someone feel unsafe, so they are unlikely to answer truthfully.

Be curious and use reciprocity. "I noticed you chose the vegetarian option. I am not a vegetarian, but I sometimes choose vegetarian food because I think it looks tastier than the meat options. What made you choose it today?" This could be a way to approach this conversation.

I am not a vegetarian, but I do want to cut down on my meat consumption for environmental reasons and will often choose vegetarian or fish options.

Once you have delved further than actions, you start to understand motives, beliefs and attitudes and are on the journey to deeper understanding.

What is critical to explore is a range of issues, especially when connected to work.

We are motivated by various aspects at work, and truly understanding what motivates difficult people requires us to explore a range of topics.

First, there are business goals. We are motivated by measures, goals, and targets that we set. Managers and leaders use these key elements to define success, and they define objectives day by day.

Second are personal attitudes and beliefs, our values and hopes. These elements include how we want to be viewed by colleagues and customers, our status amongst others and our reputation in general.

Finally, there are the politics of the business, the way departments interact, who influences us directly and indirectly, the culture of the business and business strategies.

All three of these aspects influence how we are motivated and engaged.

An easy way to understand how they might interact is to consider booking a holiday.

I am an active person who loves history and good food. I also enjoy the sunshine and being by the coast.

When I want to book a holiday, the first consideration is the commercial aspects, how much of a budget I have, how long I have available, and when I want to go.

Next, I focus on my personal beliefs and preferences, seeking a location that offers me sunshine, history, great food, activities, and somewhere I haven't been before.

If I were only concerned about my commercial limitations and personal preferences, then life would be much easier, but I am not. Like everyone else, I am influenced by the politics around me.

Other stakeholders are involved, and they have different preferences, agendas, and needs, and they have different levels of influence over my choice.

Other people coming on the holiday also have attitudes, beliefs, hopes and aspirations.

As we explore the personal needs of difficult people at work, we explore all these elements, their goals and measures, personal values and preferences and the environment that they are working within.

Only by exploring the full picture can we hope to understand their motives, and when we understand the full picture, it is much easier to empathise with them.

Empathy is a powerful asset when it comes to difficult people because it enables us to understand more about their actions and behaviours.

Empathy tools, such as labelling, become tools that help us connect with people and build trust. Labelling is a simple technique for demonstrating listening and encouraging greater depth of sharing.

During a conversation with someone, we pay attention to how they describe a situation, and we frame a question using a feeling.

For example, imagine you are talking to a customer who is describing how their system crashed a few days ago. Labelling means that you might react by suggesting, "That must have been very frustrating?"

Their reaction will either confirm your assumption, illustrating your empathy, or they will say no, giving you the chance to ask, "How did it feel?"

The end result is the same: By paying attention and using labelling, you were able to understand more about their feelings towards the system crash.

Through curiosity and an open mind, combined with the skills to label feelings and use reciprocity, it is possible to create a much deeper understanding of the goals, beliefs, attitudes, politics, and culture of difficult people. This boosts any trusted relationship you are trying to build and could be the difference between a clash of personalities and a shared understanding of priorities and pressures.

Shared Goals & Value

We are immediately suspicious of people when we are unsure of their motives. We fear being exploited, taken advantage of, made a fool of, or conned, which often prevents us from buying products from people we don't know.

Ebay, one of the early success stories of the internet for shopping, had to overcome the fear of fraud from its customers.

An online marketplace would only be successful if everyone felt safe enough to pay money and post products to people they did not know. The major role of eBay was to create this trusted environment for buying and selling and ensure that as few people as possible were defrauded.

They did it using a combination of solutions, including using PayPal to manage transactions, creating profiles that can review each other, and using a meditation service where complaints could be managed.

Since then, the internet has proliferated, and the number of sites where we can buy and sell with confidence has exploded to a point where we are now prepared to stay in other people's homes via Airbnb and share a car with strangers via Uber and Bolt.

A feeling that we are not going to be robbed is fundamental for a commercial relationship, but this fundamental fear is less of a problem in ongoing relationships.

Because of contracts and the financial and legal systems that surround them, businesses rarely need to worry about getting paid or having goods delivered by partners.

It is even less likely that employees or managers are going to be paid for work.

The problem of trust between businesses and colleagues is a feeling that there is an imbalance of value and that one party is gaining more than the other.

This stems from the human value of fairness, where we expect to be treated with a degree of fairness and cooperation by those around us. We do not need the value to be split evenly, but we do anticipate a reasonable share.

An exercise has been researched in detail by psychologists to help illustrate this phenomenon.

Two people sit opposite each other across a table. There is a proposer and a responder, and at stake is £100.

There is a time limit of 15 seconds during which a single proposal can be made by the proposer to the responder. The responder can only accept or reject this proposal; there is no opportunity to make a counterproposal.

The proposer must suggest how the £100 is divided between the two parties. They can make any proposal they want, but the decision is made by the responder who agrees or rejects the proposal.

If the responder accepts the proposal, then both parties receive the money; if they reject the proposal, then neither party gets anything.

The majority of proposers suggest an even share of 50/50, and some will make a suggestion that is in their favour, such as 60/40, 70/30, or even 80/20.

Responders will usually accept 50/50 splits and mostly accept any split, even as low as 80/20, in favour of the proposer, but once the proposer crosses this threshold, it is more likely that the responder will reject the suggestion.

If the proposer suggests 85/15 or 90/10 or worse, the responder would rather do without anything than accept something that is so obviously unfair.

Logically, this makes little sense. Any value is better than nothing, but it supports the concept that we are not logical and are driven by emotions. A feeling that the other party is gaining much more than we are, especially for nothing, creates negative feelings and causes many people to want to punish them, and themselves in the process.

It is part of the social contract to cooperate, and psychologists have been fascinated by this concept, exploring and researching a variety of variations on the game to understand it more.

What this illustrates is the importance of a sense of shared value between colleagues or customers. We can accept an imbalance, but only to a point, at which moment we feel unhappy enough to act and rebel.

It is this perceived imbalance of value that is the source of significant tension.

Difficult people may be those who appear to be demanding more than is reasonable from you. Furthermore, this definition of reasonable is open to interpretation and conflict.

In the exercise illustrated earlier, not everyone agrees that even a 50/50 split is fair, and as the balance increases in favour of one side, it is more likely to be rejected, or accepted begrudgingly.

A difficult customer or colleague might begrudgingly accept proposals so that the deal is closed, but not with trust intact, because they had no choice other than to accept.

There are very personal opinions on how value should be divided between parties, and often conflict exists because this division is judged badly by one party.

It is further complicated by the fact that the status changes over time.

Consider your first job.

In my first corporate job with a salary and benefits, I was employed as a contract salesperson on a fixed term for 9 months.

I earned £15,000 per year, and coming from professional sports, which were paid exclusively on commission, if we didn't win, we didn't get paid, it was a great position.

However, as my experience increased, I built success and became more ambitious, and that salary was no longer enough.

On territory one day, I was approached by another representative from Lundbeck. He invited me to an interview with his manager for a role in their company.

In a hotel in Manchester, we talked about the position, a full-time role with a salary of £21,000 and a BMW. I sat in a comfortable chair in the lobby, sipping a coffee, and I felt like I was in a dream.

The salary and benefits from my current company no longer satisfied me; I was worth more, and I felt undervalued by them.

I called my boss from the phone in the bedroom at my parents' house. These were the days before mobile phones, and I wanted to talk on the landline in privacy. I explained the offer and that I wanted to take it, so I waited for a counteroffer.

All she could offer was the promise of a full-time contract and a pay review in the next few months. I felt like she had listened and was going to match the offer when the time was right.

A few months later, I was given a pay review, and my salary increased to £18,000!

I was upset!

How could they undervalue me, I thought, and I was angry with myself because the other offer was gone!

I felt that trust had been breached, and they were taking more value from me than I was getting.

Years later, as a business leader, I saw the other side of the situation and saw a different story. I saw young representatives who were demanding more than they deserved.

Recently, a friend of mine was leading a commercial team in an agency and was frustrated by the number of young staff members who felt able to demand more money or threaten to leave.

He felt like they were untrustworthy because they were demanding more than they deserved and were disloyal.

Prices and commercial contracts fit into this category of value judgement.

An initial contract could present a great opportunity to a customer, and they are prepared to accept terms that, over time, and as they grow in stature, become more and more unacceptable.

Relationships that start off well can sour over time as this perception of value changes, and one party becomes more and more disillusioned.

What it means is that communication of value, perceived value, market changes and the intangible elements of value are essential to trust building.

Difficult people might feel that the value is imbalanced, they are getting a poor deal and want to shift the balance or take steps to punish you in the same way as the participants in the game did.

Sometimes this element causes parties to take radical action, even self-harming, in an attempt to prove that things must change. Unless you are able to disarm them and communicate value, there is a risk of escalation.

A perception of imbalanced value could be a driver for a difficult person who wants to feel important and special; their ego becomes a barrier in the situation, and they become frustrated.

Credibility & Empowerment

We all want to do business with the right person, someone able to help us.

Have you ever made a complaint at a hotel and demanded to see the manager or a supervisor? Why was it important to talk to a manager or a person in authority? The answer is often because when we want something to change, we need to know that the person we are talking to has the power to make it change.

There is no point asking for a refund from an employee who does not have the authority to grant one. There is no reason to ask for more information about a menu from someone who is new and doesn't know the ingredients.

Empowerment and credibility are fundamental for positive working relationships.

At one point, I was negotiating an agreement with a customer. They were an important customer, and the overall relationship was positive. A problem arose when the person who normally agreed supplier contracts was away from the business on long-term leave and the team had made interim arrangements.

They had decided that a more junior person would meet with me to discuss the deal, but would report all the discussion to a much more senior person for decision-making.

The practicalities of such an arrangement meant that I attended a meeting to present and discuss my terms, expecting a conversation. What happened was that I delivered all my proposals, the person I met with wrote everything down and then concluded the meeting.

They had nothing to say because they were under strict instructions not to do anything that was not first approved by the executive.

I was furious and immediately called their executive.

"Why are you wasting my time?" I demanded. He responded that he was giving the junior team member the chance to negotiate terms; it was a development opportunity.

I said that it wasn't because we were not allowed to discuss anything of note, and that if his plan was to approve everything, then it would be better to meet with me directly.

He understood my position and did indeed empower his team member.

Challenging the status quo can be a powerful tool when done with respect. I am proud to say that this customer, both the senior executive and the junior staff member, continues to be connected with me, and we are on very positive terms. They have engaged me to work with them as clients, a testament to building respect.

Disempowering people can be a highly damaging tactic that undermines trust and can engineer difficult customers who want to be able to talk to the right people.

At times, we disempower ourselves through a lack of confidence, a lack of preparation or through communicating badly about our level of understanding.

We are in charge of our brand image and the levels of expertise and empowerment that we communicate say much about us and the relationships we have with difficult people around us.

If you portray a lack of credibility through knowledge, expertise and empowerment, then people will not want to work with you, and it will become difficult.

The impact can be profound.

Practice is a key part of the planning process that I use with clients. It was something that is expected in sports, music, and performance, but for some reason, it is often forgotten in business.

Could you imagine paying £100 to buy tickets to a musical at a large theatre in the West End of London? You arrive to witness the bright lights of Piccadilly Circus, the bustle of the street and the restaurant where you grab a pre-dinner meal with wine before heading to the show. When you arrive at the theatre, you are told by the staff that the cast have not rehearsed the show, but do not worry, because they have been acting and singing for many years and they know what they are doing!

The show would be a disaster. The cast would not know their lines, the timing would be off and the songs out of tune.

We would demand our money back and rightly so!

Yet many people in business assume that because they have been in the role for many years, they no longer need to practice for big events.

Practice gives confidence, practice builds credibility because it allows you to learn, develop and evolve from what doesn't work well, so that during the actual meeting you are polished and sharp.

In a practice session one afternoon, I was allowing a team to run through the details of a final negotiation meeting with their largest customer.

The customer had demanded significant price cuts to their biggest brand, and my client had no choice but to comply or risk significant penalties.

At the end of the discussion, I set it that the person taking the role of the customer would accept a proposal delivered by my client. I wanted to demonstrate to them a huge risk in their plan.

At the moment the customer accepted, the team thanked them for doing so and then explained that now they would need to go back to the office and confirm the offer with leadership.

The customer was confused. "You just made the offer, I accepted it, are you saying your leadership doesn't know, or doesn't approve? Are you going to back out of this deal? They demanded, getting angry. "

The customer had not been primed, and this was a natural reaction to the initial plan of my client to take everything away to the leaders to be approved.

What they learned during the practice was that this approach could damage trust and undermine the team.

I had guessed that would happen, but the best way to learn is through experience, and that experience caused the client to immediately demand the empowerment to agree to a certain scope in the meeting, with the caveat of agreeing in writing later.

Their leadership agreed and empowered the group.

You are in charge of your personal brand, and constantly deferring to more senior people, asking others or experts to explain or support you during meetings, undermines trust in you.

If you are not projecting a certain level of confidence and personal accountability to your manager and your customers and colleagues, then they will not trust you.

If you do not trust yourself to be seen as an expert, who will?

There are frameworks within which we are able to operate, and empowerment is not unlimited, but it is harmful to be too cautious and disempower yourself.

Take opportunities to lead conversations, answer questions, publish articles, add comments or make presentations that will help support your credibility and your authority as a person who should be respected.

Respect is earned from ensuring that what you say is credible and delivered with confidence, and it is that combination that helped me to earn the respect of my customers, a respect that endures many years later.

Consistency

When I ask people about trust and what it means, a common response is connected to consistency.

We build trust with people over time based on our experiences, and we learn to trust expectations of behaviour that are predictable.

We can trust people who are unreliable, because they are always that way. My dad was always late, everywhere. He consistently underestimated how long the travel time would be and overestimated how much he could complete in the time he had.

He was reliably unreliable!

It meant that whenever we planned to go anywhere, we lied about the time we needed to leave so that we had a chance of him being ready in time.

Consistency is not the need for people to be reliable per se; rather, it is the need for us to know what to expect. Unpredictability creates uncertainty, and that creates fear.

Imagine you had a daughter who regularly goes out with friends on a Thursday evening after work. Each week, she tells you that she will have a couple of drinks and arrive home at about 9 pm. However, each week she sends a message at 8 pm to say that she is going to be much later because they are going for dinner somewhere.

She is unreliable, but consistently so and as such, there is an element of trust.

You would never trust her to come home on time, and should there be an important event one Thursday evening that you need her to attend, and she promises to be there, you would not be confident that she will show up because of the history.

If she does show up on time one Thursday evening as promised, you are likely to be surprised, but pleasantly surprised. However, you cannot now trust her reliability and consistency, and her promises to be home on time. It was one occasion after many disappointments, and it takes time to prove reliability.

Working with people, we need consistency and reliability so we can predict behaviours.

If we have a manager who consistently speaks to staff about lateness, even if they do not show any flexibility, we trust that they will be consistent, and that gives us comfort. We know what will happen when we arrive at the office late.

At work, we build trust with people who keep promises, who are dependable when they agree to complete a task and who can even be relied upon to follow through on threats that they make.

I have many clients who want to appear confident and assertive during commercial deals. They want to make threats to their customers in order to create leverage during commercial discussions.

I warn them of the risks.

The problem with making a threat is that you need to carry it out if they do not comply with your demands; failure to do so reduces the level of trust they have in you. Should you decide to make a threat in the future, they will no longer take that threat seriously.

A client of mine was negotiating the price of a key medicine with one of their largest customers. There were some very senior people in a meeting discussing possible strategies, and they had started discussions over breakfast before I arrived at the meeting. They were very pleased with their idea.

I walked into a large hotel conference room set out with an array of buffet breakfast options, fruit and scrambled eggs, plus a choice of coffee, tea and juices laid out on long tables at the side.

In the centre were circular tables set for 8, where the team were sitting, drinking coffee, and munching pastries.

As I sat down with my plate and began to eat, they announced that they wanted to discuss the 'exploding suitcase strategy' with me.

This was their idea to create leverage on this large customer.

The plan was simple, a highly tempting offer, one that was too good to be true, but that only existed for 24 hours before expiring.

Using this plan, they intended to kick out the competition and secure a larger share of the business for themselves.

I asked them, "What happens if the customer waits longer than 24 hours and then responds to say yes?" "Hmmm", they wondered. "What if they call back in three days and say that they will not kick out the competition, but they want the price you have quoted, or they will kick you out?" "Hmmm", they replied again.

I knew that my client was not prepared to carry out any threats against this customer. They were too large to risk conflict and lost business.

There was also a history of fake threats where my client had failed to carry out threats, and as such, the customer was already confident that any time limits were not real.

On the other hand, the customer was prepared to issue and execute threats to kick out key brands. My client was afraid that by using the strategy, they might create a situation where they could lose significantly.

The client decided against the 'exploding suitcase strategy' simply because they weren't prepared to impose the threat, and they would have demonstrated to the customer a price that they could accept, which was much lower than they intended to agree to.

In all, making a threat they were not prepared to carry out, combined with revealing terms that they didn't want to have to agree to, was too risky.

Difficult people are frequently so because they are inconsistent.

They fail to do what they promise, a colleague who volunteers for a project and then doesn't do their part, a manager who makes promises about rewards and recognition that never appear, or customers who promise to send purchase orders, but they do not arrive.

They may also be suspicious of you if you do the same.

It can be easy to make promises and raise threats at certain moments, but by doing so, you are creating problems later when they do not arrive.

Making staff feel special and then not elevating them somehow is risky; making demands of customers and issuing specific threats might work in the short term, but in time, they will become tired of the same threats and perhaps call your bluff.

Your level of consistency requires careful reflection, like the other aspects of trust, and an honest look.

Failing to see the world as the people around you see it could cause you to miss areas where you are the problem and have been inconsistent.

Even if you are reliable, you are not the only face your customers and colleagues see. Their impression of your business is made up of a network of interactions and engagements, and if they are disappointed by the service and experience of any of them, that could be enough to damage trust with you and your business.

Vulnerability & Humility

Do you have all the answers? Are you someone who is very confident in their ability to deliver excellent results? Do you need help from anyone to do your job well? Have you seen it all before?

There is a fine line between confidence and arrogance.

Confident people know their strengths and have faith in their ability to deliver results, but they also know their limitations and where they need help and support.

Arrogant people have self-belief but lack awareness of shortcomings and failings. They have problems that they are unaware of that can hold them back.

I played rugby with a guy who has gone on to have a highly successful career as a strength and conditioning coach, first in rugby and later in the US with American Football.

He is a highly self-confident person and has been accused by many people of being arrogant.

As a young man, he was selling strength programmes to rugby players alongside his playing to make money, and he has always been very forthright in his views.

There are many very experienced strength coaches across the sport, and he has always been confident to debate, challenge, question and even argue with them on technical points.

On face value, it could appear that he was incredibly arrogant. A young guy with little professional experience challenging some of the top coaches in the world.

But what they didn't know was how hard he worked, how much reading he did and how carefully he studied.

He was confident because he knew the details of the latest research and was able to recite both modern and older techniques, debating their relative merits.

A phrase he used often that has stayed with me is "it is only arrogance if you can't deliver"

We like to work with confident people who reassure us that they know what they are doing, and we can trust their judgment.

Confident people are unafraid of questions and will encourage others to share ideas and make suggestions. They are self-assured enough not to feel threatened by other people with different ideas, and they will be open to hearing differing opinions and defend their position where necessary.

We fear working with arrogant people because we anticipate that they will not listen to our ideas, be open to new ways of working, make incorrect assumptions, and not be open about where they need help.

Confidence is attractive, arrogance is not.

In 2010, Jose Mujica was elected as president of Uruguay. When he was elected, Uruguay was suffering from a series of challenges, including poverty and inequality, access to healthcare and education and access to infrastructure such as energy and communications.

He brought with him a very different type of leadership, one that is associated with humility.

He donated 90% of his presidential salary to charity, lived in a modest farmhouse and drove an old VW Beetle.

His approach resonated strongly with the population and connected him deeply to their struggles.

During his presidency, he was successful in reducing poverty from over 39% to less than 11% and extreme poverty from 5% to less than 0.5%.

He emphasised economic stability, social equality and a just society and built a reputation for Uruguay as one of the most progressive countries in Latin America.

Humility can be a powerful contributor to trust and inspire positive change. It creates an environment where people become accessible, curious and part of a larger group dedicated to delivering something special.

When you are vulnerable, you are able to admit that you do not have all the answers. This admission encourages others to share ideas and breaks down internal walls.

A lack of vulnerability is a key factor for difficult people who cannot admit that they are wrong and need to change their strategy. They are more likely to ignore timely advice and alternative options, they will reject details they have not thought of, and they will refuse to ask questions.

Curiosity is one of the most powerful assets a company can possess, and cultivating a curious culture adds significantly to the business performance.

The book "The Curiosity Manifesto" by Stefaan van Hooydonk explores the power of curiosity for businesses and describes it as the secret ingredient for success.

To be curious requires humility, and humility is lacking with people who refuse to be vulnerable.

We do not trust people who appear too perfect, who cannot admit mistakes, are not open to learn and who remain fixed in the belief that they know best.

When we are building trusted partnerships at work, we seek people who are adaptable, imaginative and flexible. These traits require vulnerability.

At the start of the section, I posed a series of questions about you and your openness to learn.

The answers to these questions suggest a lot about your level of vulnerability. How willing are you to change your mind, be open to new ways of working, and ensure that you have practised and worked hard to prepare?

If you feel that you do not need to adapt, change, learn, evolve, grow, practice and develop, then you could be lacking in vulnerability.

If you consider with whom you are willing to admit these things when they do exist, these are the people with whom you feel safe enough to be vulnerable.

If you have these traits, but save them for certain situations, then you are likely to hinder the levels of trust with those you are not prepared to be more open with.

Vulnerability, like personal needs, is something that we can share and reciprocate. We need to feel safe enough to open up, and as such, there are layers through which we pass to build trust over time.

Making a start, showing areas of vulnerability, asking for feedback and encouraging others to do the same are powerful tools to build trust in a group.

A colleague of mine explained the concept of reciprocal mentoring as a powerful tool for this purpose.

It works by connecting people across siloes, or perhaps across grades or functions. The goal is that within an hour session, both parties in attendance have the opportunity to be a mentor and mentee.

Each brings something to discuss that they want to get a perspective, help or advice with, and they share ideas.

It takes time, but the results are amazing. It breaks down barriers between departments and functions, encouraging a culture of mutual support and sharing. Contrary to the usual format of mentoring, it is bi-directional, which reduces any feelings of supe-riority and demands humility and vulnerability.

SEE THE WORLD THROUGH THEIR EYES

Trust is a central theme to understand where problems exist with difficult people. We can use the elements of trust to diagnose what is going wrong and take steps to strengthen areas where there are gaps.

When I engage clients and explore issues surrounding the difficult people they are trying to work with, exploring various elements of trust is an excellent starting point.

Trust levels across the various elements provide a benchmark for the status of the relationship and set some goals for what needs to change in order to improve the situation.

If you do not understand enough about what motivates them, what they are worried about and what they aspire to, you can invest time exploring these areas.

Suppose you feel that they do not take you seriously as a credible person. In that case, you can build your profile and personal brand by being more active in communicating your knowledge and expe-rience and taking responsibility for decision-making.

If you feel they do not have faith in you to deliver your promises, you can acknowledge issues and take steps to provide them with assurances or add warranties to agreements.

Suppose you think that you seem arrogant or that they do not feel secure enough to be open with you about their areas of weakness. In that case, you can initiate some conversations using reciprocity to slowly build a stronger sense of transparency.

These steps are all important, but are impossible unless you can really understand how they see you and how they see the world around them.

We See What We Want to See

When we engage with the world, we see everything through the filters of our beliefs and experiences. We do not see things as they are, but as we interpret them based on who we are.

As we evolve, change and grow, our circumstances and experiences change, and how we might interpret actions will change along with them.

Difficult people at work are not trying to be difficult. They are working towards their goals, escaping their fears and doing so in ways they believe are the right way to make the fastest progress.

They are influenced by the culture they evolved in, the people around them, and dozens of other factors.

The culture of some countries is individualistic, and the culture of others is collective. This is not a reflection of politics, but an imprint of years of evolution.

An individualistic culture operates where the feelings, goals, and fears of the individual are central. It is likely to focus on success at a personal level and pay little heed to the performance of the group unless it directly affects the individual's outcomes.

Hard work will be rewarded by personal gain, and those who do not work hard are more likely to be rejected.

In collective cultures, the success of the group is more important than the individual, and individuals will be expected to make personal sacrifices for the collective good.

Toyota is the world's largest car maker with a reputation for producing high-quality vehicles. They were pioneers of manufacturing processes of high efficiency and accuracy that have been spread around the world and inspired hundreds of industries to work in now ways.

One of the elements that helped create their high-performance systems was that when an error was found on the manufacturing line, the whole process was stopped while the problem was identified and fixed.

Groups of people would work together to understand the weaknesses of the whole system and focus not just on the specific problem, but on the causation, which might sit elsewhere in the system.

Engineers were encouraged to proactively raise mistakes that they made in order to highlight problems in the system that weaken the whole process.

This is a wonderful example of collectivism.

It is understood that a problem for one is a problem for everyone, and as such, everyone needs to share, explore and repair problems so that everyone gains in the end.

A similar scenario occurs in the aircraft industry, where safety is the number one priority.

Pilots and crew who witness near misses are protected from blame, regardless of fault, if they proactively report the incident.

The only goal is to identify weak points in the system, not assign blame. When weaknesses are spotted, they can be repaired before a serious accident occurs.

Accidents damage the whole industry with respect to trust in flying and passenger numbers, as well as the cost of destroyed and damaged aircraft and passenger deaths.

Collectivism places the whole at the centre, and the individuals are less important than the success of the whole. Using this system enables businesses and industries to create robust, safe and efficient systems that deliver high-performance organisations.

Individualistic cultures place individuals at the centre of the business, rewarding creativity, performance and results for each person.

They create a competitive environment where success is based on the brilliance of each person, adding up to a collective performance.

In these cultures, an equal measure of hope for success and fear of failure exists. People invest to stand out and take risks to deliver results, but they must also fear the consequences of mistakes.

On a manufacturing line, workers would be rewarded for the amount they deliver, and failing to meet quotas would be punished. In addition, problems that they discover might be blamed on them, creating a culture where shifting responsibility for failings to others becomes valuable.

In recent years, one of the world's leading aircraft manufacturers, Boeing, has been beset by problems and issues with manufacturing and safety.

The poor quality of their safety standards and engineering has resulted in a series of fatal crashes and the grounding of aircraft.

Workers during the ensuing investigations have reported that warnings of safety concerns were ignored by managers, and a culture of blame was created where workers became afraid of raising issues.

They do not have a highly efficient and effective manufacturing production line, perhaps because they have a more individualistic culture.

There are merits to both of these cultures, and drawbacks to them, too.

What is important to understand is that difficult people are a product of their past and their culture.

A person from a collective culture, working in an individualistic world, will struggle to understand the decision-making processes, the people around them and ways of working.

They will be judged as difficult because the ideas they suggest will be totally different to what is expected from the majority.

However, they will not understand the problem because they work collectively and do not understand why others do not.

The problem of seeing the world through your eyes is the fundamental challenge to overcome when trying to work with difficult people.

In my workshops, I present clients with an image to consider.

It is a set of stairs reaching high up a wall to the next floor in a building. Sitting at the bottom, empty is a wheelchair, with the words "If you were sitting in the chair, what would you be thinking?"

It is a stark, challenging and powerful image that evokes an emotional reaction.

The responses to the challenge usually include the question of 'how am I going to get up there?', yet the answer for the majority of people in the room is clear: the stairs.

However, stairs do not work for people who need to use a wheelchair, people with limited mobility, parents with children, or people carrying bags.

There are dozens of exceptions to the rule that stairs are the best way to get to the next floor of a building.

The problem is that often designers of buildings are able-bodied, fit and healthy and simply do not see a need for another option.

It is taking legislation to change the way buildings are created to increase accessibility, and yet, we would all benefit from ramps, escalators, lifts, moving walkways and the other systems that exist to help mobility. These tools are not for the exclusive benefit of people with limitations.

Too often, when we are thinking of solutions to problems, we can only consider ideas from our perspective.

I travelled to Greece recently with a colleague to work with a client. We were helping them to plan for the launch of a line of skincare products into pharmacies in Europe.

One of the tasks that we brought to the group was a challenge to consider a customer journey and a customer profile.

We wanted them to explore the hopes, fears and experiences of their customers and to consider how they would help solve their problems.

The focus was not on the consumer seeking improved skin health, but on the retailer whom they were trying to influence to stock the range of products.

We sat in a Greek restaurant in a back street of Athens and discussed our plans for the next day over plates of delicious grilled fish and vegetables.

He told me a story that perfectly illustrates the problem of seeing the world through our own eyes.

He said that he was once working on a healthcare brand for pain as a category director.

His team did some research into consumer profiling. They wanted to explore the buying journey and the various triggers.

As a group, they defined 2-3 consumer profiles that would be ideal consumers of the brand. He said that each profile they described was a professional male or female, aged 25-35, who worked in an office and led a busy and active life. Some had children, some didn't.

Nothing wrong with the profiles, he said, on face value, they seemed reasonable enough, until he looked up from the documents and around the table.

Sitting around the table were a group of males and females aged 25-35 who were professionals, living busy lifestyles, some with and some without children.

They had described themselves!

This is so common.

The starting point for many of my client engagements is descriptions of difficult customers. Analysis and exploration tell me quickly that there is a clash of expectations and a lack of understanding.

At one point, a large client brought me in to support a team that was struggling with discount retail customers in the UK.

The team explained to me that the customers were chaotic.

Whenever they arrived at the office, they could see people running around, on the phones, and various examples of stock lying around. They complained of the lack of firm plans and demands for discounts, exclusives, and special packs.

They lamented the ordering process, the challenges they face from supply chain colleagues who struggle to manage orders and deliver to multiple locations.

It was a nightmare, they explained, and these customers were impossible.

The reason they wanted my help was that this channel was a high-growth channel in the market, and leadership demanded that the team find a way to unlock the opportunity.

As I explored the issues surrounding the difficulties, it became obvious to me where the problem was.

The discounter operated in a world where they relished and embraced flexibility and adaptability. Their stock was not fixed, and their strategy was to find opportunities to offer something cheap and relevant to customers.

They needed special packs, low prices, exclusives, and seasonality because their model demanded them.

If the weather gets warm in April, they want to be first to offer cheap barbecues, garden furniture, and water guns to take advantage of the opportunity.

They operate a last-minute, high-intensity business that is commit-ted to finding deals fast, seeing what sells and buying more until they discover the next opportunity.

The buyers were chaotic and late to meetings because they were on the phone trying to find suppliers and buy stock that was needed immediately.

This culture was completely alien to my client.

They worked in a highly structured and highly forecasted manner. Their customers planned a year ahead and had clear sales forecasts that could be passed to manufacturing and supply chains.

They were efficient, with a limited choice of range and kept wastage to a minimum.

These two cultures were incompatible, and to make a success of working together would require deeper understanding and changes from one side or the other.

This example illustrates perfectly the twin issues at the heart of difficult people and succeeding with them.

A customer who is difficult because of their culture and ways of working, but who does not intend to be so.

Overcoming the challenge is a potential business opportunity, and a competitive advantage comes from those who are able to adapt and overcome the issues, but to do so requires the business to understand and adapt.

All of this is uncomfortable and challenging. It is exactly these reasons that make succeeding with difficult people hard.

In this case, to fully exploit the opportunity would require my client to deal with this channel of customers in a different way.

They need to be prepared for unpredictable sales, have a range of products designed for the discount channel, and build a delivery network that is able to service more service centres.

If this is not possible, then there is value available through better understanding and acknowledging that the customer works differently and isn't trying to be difficult.

Knowing that asking them to forecast months in advance is going to be impossible, recognising that they want special pricing and they don't want to be fobbed off with products that don't sell in other channels, will help unlock more trust and better results.

Success with difficult people relies on the ability to see the world through their eyes and understanding that they are not trying to be difficult.

There are some tools that can help you make this critical leap.

First, focus on an individual that you want to better understand. Create some key headings that you are going to research. These are personal objectives, business culture and personal beliefs.

It might seem like a difficult task, but it is incredible how much can be learned through research and general conversations.

Explore their targets, goals, measures and aspirations at work. This will help you understand their personal objectives, elements that the business expects from them and therefore what they will need to achieve to feel successful.

Consider the business they work for. What are the business objectives, how do they work, communicate, and what are their values? Do they have specific processes they follow, and how do they feel about taking risks, and how open are they to adopting and implementing change?

This will shape the freedom they have to try new things, make decisions and operate differently.

Once you understand their goals and their environment, consider them as a personality.

How do they communicate, how do they react to authority, what are their values, and who are their key connections?

Through all this research, you will have a detailed map of what and how they work, giving you a lot of insight into areas that you will find difficult to work with.

Finally, ask yourself how important it is that you succeed with this person. It is essential you appreciate the effort and the results you will achieve because being successful with this person could be uncomfortable, require you to change, and reset your approach to aspects that you value.

They are difficult because you are struggling with them, and changing them is hard.

Overcoming some barriers requires persistence and patience, and it might feel like writing with your less preferred hand.

The elephant in the room is often the fact that if you asked them what they think of you, I suspect that they would say that you are difficult.

From their point of view, it is you who is not behaving the way they want. If there is conflict and tension, they will argue that you are the one who is causing it.

It is easy to sit and blame others, and that is what you will both do.

It is a wonderful way to explain why things are bad, "because it is their fault".

One of my first clients told me the problem was the customer who was 'being difficult'.

When we talked more, it was obvious that his company was trying to impose ways of thinking on the customer, and they were trying to act differently.

The customer was not difficult; they had a different way of working, and that created a clash.

But is it more comfortable to blame them? It is more convenient to make them accountable.

But that will not solve anything.

This book is designed to encourage you to reflect on yourself, realise that there is a problem, and take steps to change.

When you accept that you are the one in control of your actions, behaviours and the relationships you have, then you can take control of the difficult people and find ways to resolve the problem.

Stop getting angry.

Reflect on what you need, be patient during meetings, be curious to understand where the issues lie and then be prepared to find answers through taking accountability for change.

BEING UNCOMFORTABLE

"Is the juice worth the squeeze?"

That is what an associate often asks when we are working on projects together.

Whenever we engage in a programme, we are seeking to get results from the effort and hard work. If the amount of effort we need to make in order to deliver results is too great, then perhaps it isn't worth the extra work?

When clients call me to deal with difficult customers, the value is most definitely there.

Frequently, these are customers who are large and deliver significant value for my clients, and the difficulties are emerging over time because of changes in personnel or because of increasing demands.

Own the Moral High Ground

I spent 5 years working with a large client in the US on a regular basis. They have a few very large, very powerful buyers in their marketplace, and these buyers have become very skilled in leveraging value from them, and they wanted to turn the tide.

The organisation found itself constantly being held to ransom by these customers who threatened to remove their brands from sale unless they offered more value.

The business was not prepared to take the risk of rejecting the demands and then losing the sale value because of the impact on the share price of the whole business.

What they wanted to be able to do was to shift the relationship to build the credibility of the team, leverage the power they did have and build respect so that they could resist constant demands for value.

It has taken 5 years of supporting and advising a series of complex negotiations, but the relationship is in a different place than it was.

The team is now confident and practised, able to stand their ground even against high-pressure tactics.

We have totally changed a few aspects of strategy and positioning, we have been much clearer on proposals and the messages that we send in what and when we propose, and the team are well prepared with arguments to illustrate and defend positions.

My client now owns the identity of good partners, a special customer who should be treated differently from other suppliers, and we use strategies that are consistent across the portfolio.

For example, there are sometimes opportunities to exclude competitor brands in certain categories through the deals that are done.

These are tempting for my client, their leadership love the idea of excluding competition and growing market share. It creates attractive headlines for them and gives them recognition from executives.

The problem is that excluding competitors is very expensive. The amount of value that must be invested is significant, but what is more expensive is that it rarely lasts, and yet the value is hard to recover because a new bar is set.

Additionally, in other categories where my client is less strong, other brands can exclude theirs, offsetting gains on one with losses on another.

Instead, we have implemented a strategy of never excluding competitors and refusing to participate in bids to do so.

My client owns the position that consumers get to make the choice of products, and their marketing teams will be able to differentiate the brands. Their role with the customer is simply to make sure they are available when the decision is made.

This strategy is part of the big picture, which is to become less competitive, aggressive, and assertive.

Instead, the team is balanced, cautious and pragmatic.

We removed the emotional reactions and personality clashes and separated the decision from the person.

In the past, 'the buyer was an idiot for his threats'; today, 'we don't like the threats, but appreciate that they are doing their job'

This different view is empowering and provides my client with control of the relationship and takes much of the power of intimidation away from the difficult customer.

But it has not been easy.

Normalise the Abnormal

It doesn't matter if you are someone who is more comfortable with a focus on results or someone who is naturally inclined to think about relationships; when challenged to reset the balance and become more of the other, it will be uncomfortable.

This discomfort is an essential part of success with difficult people.

We have a choice, either to be uncomfortable with meeting them because we dislike the experience, or uncomfortable because we are doing something differently to find new ways to be successful.

I think it is an easy choice.

When you take action to find a solution to a difficult problem, you are taking control of the situation and making something positive happen. This is especially true, knowing that there is a business advantage available when you do.

All the successful people I have met are prepared to make themselves uncomfortable to achieve success. It is a prerequisite for success.

I think that one of the major factors that makes someone outstanding is their ability to normalise the abnormal.

If they can regularly perform the actions and tasks that others see as special, then they are going to become outstanding.

I have witnessed this many times through my career, and it appears in many forms, but it is always uncomfortable.

As a rugby league player, I have stood in dressing rooms before matches, looking around the room at others who were nervous about what was about to happen.

Rugby league is a confrontational and physical game. It involves significant collisions and a risk of injury. This is on top of the importance of certain matches like cup finals and play-off games.

There is much at stake, both physically and emotionally, as well as financial incentives.

Pressure weighs heavily on the faces of the people in the dressing room, and it is easy to see.

Everyone carries some degree of nerves and fear. There is uncertainty, hopes, worries and expectations.

The greatest players are those who understand this and rise to the occasion. They rebrand nerves to excitement, turning stress into adrenaline they can use.

I have witnessed some incredible achievements of physical endurance. I have seen players complete matches with fractured cheekbones and leave the field to receive stitches in wounds before returning to complete the game.

Personally, I have replaced dislocated fingers while never leaving the field, and I strapped up my knee with tape to protect a snapped ligament so that I could play in key matches.

It is the same in the office.

I know people who work very hard, and normalise preparation that others feel is excessive. But they are always fully prepared.

As humans, we are naturally inclined to find a shortcut. Many inventions are successful because they make tasks easier and save effort and time.

But the people who do not take shortcuts at work reap the rewards.

Difficult customers are an example of how normalising abnormal pay dividends.

Additional effort to prepare for conversations, doing research, reading around a topic or practising to build your skill and confidence will set you apart from others.

Difficult customers, colleagues and managers have become so because we often sought out shortcuts to make life easier.

When you choose to address the issues and find solutions, it is a time to recognise that it will require effort, thought, reflection and honesty.

Honesty with yourself about what your contribution has been to creating the problem, because it is a clash of people, not exclusively one person, who has created the issues.

Your choice to address the problem means you are accountable for change because it is unlikely that you are going to be able to tell them to fix themselves.

Remember, they blame you, and unless you take responsibility for change, nothing will change.

Difficult Conversations

The moment when all the thought and reflections comes to life is when you talk about difficulties with the person.

This is the crucial moment when you will need to face your fears.

It never gets easier; in the same way that sportspeople always feel nervous, performers on stage anticipate the curtain call, and you will always feel anxious before a conversation with a difficult person.

However, there are some stages to keep in mind that will help you to prepare and succeed in difficult conversations.

This is a topic that is raised often with clients, and it is something that I researched to learn some methods from people who have difficult conversations on a regular basis.

I talked to doctors who deal with cancer sufferers.

I could not think of a group that more frequently deals with difficult conversations than this group. Every day, they share news about diagnosis, prognosis and death with patients and families.

In addition, it is rare to hear complaints about the demeanour of cancer physicians. They are usually reported to be pragmatic, honest, and respectful when sharing bad news.

These are traits that I think are valuable for any difficult conversation, and as such, the lessons that they teach us are essential for us to be able to successfully address sensitive topics with difficult people at work.

There is a particular recipe that is used to help guide these difficult conversations that I share with clients to help them prepare for conversations for everything from price increases to sharing negative feedback to addressing issues with manager behaviour.

It is widely considered that difficult conversations should be a mixture of positive and negative news. This sandwich structure, with the negativity at the centre of the two pieces of positivity, is often taught as a way of delivering bad news.

I am not convinced, especially when it comes to difficult people.

There is a significant opportunity for misunderstanding and a high risk that the person hears only the positive elements.

This is a critical risk with difficult people because it is exactly this misunderstanding and misinterpretation that could be part of the problem.

You might want to deliver inspiration for change, and they hear how well they are doing.

The structure that I advocate is more direct, clearer, and unambiguous, but it is also more stressful and uncomfortable.

However, to effect change, one must embrace discomfort, and this does not mean that the conversation should be disrespectful, aggressive, or even heated.

In fact, the opposite is true. The conversation needs to be calm, controlled and thoughtful. The moment it becomes emotional is the moment when it is helpful to take a break and return later.

There are several ingredients to the methodology.

First, the scene and frame of the conversation need to be set. It is also important to choose an appropriate time and place.

Catching someone between meetings when they are busy is not respectful. It is also essential that you take the time to consider the meeting and prepare. Avoid the temptation to 'deal with issues in the moment'. You are probably responding emotionally to something that has happened, and as such, it is unlikely you will handle the situation calmly and with balance.

If you are emotional, then it is likely you will lose the moral high ground and therefore the arguments that support your opinions.

Initiate the conversation by telling the person that you want to have an important discussion with them about something that is bothering you, and you need some time.

If you can outline some general issues, then that is helpful so they can prepare. For example, if you have been thinking about some feedback for them on a topic, then tell them.

You are then giving them the chance to consider their view.

If they demand to speak immediately, then resist the temptation. They might be emotional, and it could derail the discussion before you start.

Don't wait too long, but do suggest that a later time works better.

When you start the conversation, have a simple, clear statement ready and deliver it calmly.

Practising the delivery is a helpful tactic; it helps you to feel comfortable with the words and avoid stumbling.

When you talk to someone, you absolutely cannot tell them how they felt or what they were doing.

For example, you cannot say "you were disrespectful to me" or "you were playing power games"

You cannot tell them how others were feeling unless you have specifically gathered this information. It is common for managers to talk to team members and try to provide feedback on behalf of others. For example, "Everyone was confused by your presentation"

You do not know how others feel, nor do you know their intentions. To claim you do opens up an argument about the feelings they had and shifts the conversation away from the key issues.

You can talk about how you felt, or if you have spoken to others to get insights into feelings, you can refer to these, but you need to be specific and refer only to the people you spoke with.

You can talk about what they did, the actions they took, and how it made you feel. For example, "You said that my work was of poor quality in front of my colleagues, and I felt disrespected"

In the case of feedback, you can say, "I saw your presentation and I thought it was confusing. Afterwards, I spoke to Joanne and she was also confused"

Once you have delivered your message, go silent for a few seconds to allow the other person to think and reflect.

It is likely that once they have heard your comments, they will domand more information. Be prepared.

Have to hand figures, information or examples to illustrate your point. The goal is to make your claims credible and valid, not over-whelm them with data and details.

It is this moment where preparation matters, the examples you share, and the way you explain make a huge difference.

Empathy and respect are essential. You are not trying to be aggres-sive, but be balanced and empathetic. They do not want to hear bad news, so delivering it insensitively will not help.

At this point, they are going to object and reject the arguments. Avoid the temptation to compromise or to back down.

In a cancer diagnosis, the doctor is often faced with a patient who wants a second opinion or rejects the diagnosis. The doctor does not suggest that they are wrong and argues that they hold firm. They respond that the tests have shown cancer is present and that the patient can talk to someone else if they like or ask for tests to be repeated, but that it is in their interests to start treatment.

If you have delivered your feelings and supported them with examples and evidence, then you should not back down. Simply respond, that is how you felt.

The final stage is to talk about what you need to happen next.

Consider some ideas of how you want things to change for the future.

Be future facing, demanding apologies or reparations for past deeds might feel good, but can create more conflict.

It is usually more important to agree on future actions given the same situation.

For example, in the situation where you felt disrespected, you might suggest that instead of giving you feedback in front of others in future, they do so in private to allow you to process their comments.

This structure provides you with a framework you can practice. You can practice delivering the news and sharing the examples. It is also very helpful to consider what objections and issues they will raise, and prepare answers and responses.

Practice the conversation with others ahead of time, and remember that difficult people are not fixed in one conversation.

To deliver change over time requires persistence and the capacity to have the same or similar conversations again and again.

Be patient, be uncomfortable and be calm.

Don't Say No!

Negative language damages trust and relationships.

Think of how it feels when you are in a meeting and you present ideas only for them to be rejected, one after the other.

It is demoralising.

Would you continue trying to offer ideas and answers if every time you did, you were rejected, questioned, challenged and made to feel that you were not being heard?

Of course not.

Yet, frequently we find ourselves in exactly that situation. We find people difficult when they simply reject our proposals, and we become emotional, frustrated and angry.

We may choose to raise the tension, forcing our point and raising our voices, only to escalate the situation into a full argument.

But worse is the fact that it is we who lose our temper and become emotional, and we lose the moral high ground.

When we do this, it is hard to recover.

It is for that reason that we need to remain calm and avoid arguments, escalations and emotions.

Patience and silence are our friends, and we need to learn to use them wisely.

Silence is not a power tactic, as I hear it described frequently; it is a chance to gather our thoughts and to order our words before we take the next step.

Silence is an active process, designed to provide us with the control needed to reassert ourselves in the meeting. During silence, we think and we watch, reading the body language and considering how to progress.

Reciprocity is a powerful tool of behaviour. It is the concept that we naturally want to cooperate with others, and it is a foundation of community.

One person helps another, who helps another and so on.

It is the basis for business, someone who can build a wall, cooperates with someone who can build a roof, and together they build houses. They share expertise and value.

But it also influences behaviour.

In a meeting, when one person becomes negative and tense, it can easily become infectious, and others reciprocate, creating additional tension.

No, has this effect.

When we hear no, we begin to think negatively and start to reject and protect. We reciprocate negativity with negativity.

Instead of allowing this to escalate, I have learned the importance of positive language.

Changing the words matters. When we use no, it feels final and destructive. But by carefully engineering words, we can alter the perception of what is heard and change the mood.

"No, I disagree." It is strong, assertive and negative. Associated with that statement is confidence, authority and status.

The problem is that it can kill the mood or escalate tension.

Instead, "That's interesting, but I see it differently" communicates curiosity and indicates that there is more to discuss.

Using silence, it is possible to change our mindset and shift an argument and negativity into something positive.

When tension arises and people become defensive, a well-chosen phrase can help progress the meeting.

"I can see that wo are starting to get more tense. We have made a lot of progress, and I would like to continue on a positive note. What can we do to keep progressing?"

It can be a sensitive way to reset the mood.

When your ideas are rejected, it is easy to react defensively: "You have rejected my ideas, what do you suggest we do instead?"

This is challenging and negative. It is emotional and communicates that you are becoming frustrated.

Instead, consider "I can see that my ideas are not what you are looking for right now. But I am keen to find a way to move forward. Can we discuss ways that will help us?"

This language remains balanced and open. It is receptive to discussion without conceding the point.

Tone of voice matters, and it is essential to avoid confrontation and tension.

The use of silence and control enables us to break from the moment, think positively and restructure our statements so that we encourage cooperation and increase understanding.

We should separate people from decisions.

They are not rejecting you; they don't like that idea.

They are not being difficult; they want the best for themselves

They might not like the proposal, but you can still have a good relationship.

The objective is to make the people in the meeting feel listened to and respected, but you can disagree with the points they make.

That is the essence of balancing results and relationships.

What matters is how you communicate, the tone and the words. What you communicate is less important.

Say what you want to say, in a positive and constructive way, without argument, and you will change the tone of meetings.

INFLUENCING DIFFICULT PEOPLE

Ruled by Chimps

Once you have explored issues of trust and decided to have a difficult conversation to redress the balance between results and relationships, you must find ways to influence difficult people and bring them to your way of thinking, or at least become someone they respect.

The starting point for many when it comes to influencing others is to find evidence and logic to support your arguments. We mistakenly believe that it is data that convinced us of our beliefs, and the data will be powerful enough to change the opinions of those around us. But this is far from being the case.

Contrary to what we believe, data plays only a small part in establishing our beliefs and attitudes. What matters much more are feelings.

Take climate change as an example. I believe that the planet is on a path to catastrophe, due to carbon emissions leading to global warming, and I also believe that reducing the amount of meat that humans consume is the single most powerful way we can address this issue. That is why I try to reduce the amount of meat I eat, switch to fish or choose vegetarian options.

I have come to this belief not through reading data; in fact, I have never read a single trial into the causes and effects of climate change. I have evolved this belief over the years by listening to people I respect and trusting what they say.

I cannot recount a single data point to support my belief, and have no books to recommend on the subject.

Many people do not believe as I do and challenge my beliefs. They will point to data and research that supports their arguments, but I will not be moved.

Despite never reading any, I believe that the data in my favour is overwhelming!

What does this tell us about the importance of evidence?

It suggests that reliance on evidence is going to lead to failure. In many cases, strong arguments and evidence can be provided on both sides of an argument.

Research shows that people with a strong set of beliefs are more inclined to double down on their initial thoughts when exposed to counterarguments and evidence than to take notice of the contradictory evidence.

Our decision-making system evolved well before the advanced brain we have today, and it was designed to help us survive and succeed in a world tens of thousands of years before statistical analysis was even imagined.

We learned to make decisions to help us succeed as primitive humans living in small groups, towards the middle of the food chain, where more dangerous predators hunted us.

In his book "The Chimp Paradox", Steve Peters, a psychologist known for working with elite cycling, top sports people, and very disturbed personalities, explores the separate decision-making units of the modern human brain.

He characterises three distinct parts. The chimp brain is the most primitive, most powerful and fastest part of the brain to react. The computer, where we automate decision making to save energy and time and where we programme responses and habits, and the human brain, where logic, reason, language and numbers are managed. This human brain is the weakest and slowest part of the brain to react to a situation, despite our belief to the contrary.

Steve Peters describes the system as designed in this way because of when it was built. We have learned and invented ways to dominate the planet too quickly for biology to keep up. As a result, we have brains built for survival in a world that no longer exists.

Our brains are emotional, reactive and habitual. We learn and develop through experiences, and fears are powerful lessons that we find hard to forget.

The common fear of speaking in public is not a logical assessment of the difficulties of remembering words. It is a complex combination of worries about how others might reject us for making mistakes, a fear of judgement, and being cast out by others we rely on for support, security and status.

Steve Peters describes the demands of the chimp part of our brains being connected to the importance of living in a community for survival.

We have evolved a fear of isolation, a fear of rejection and a fear of being judged as different because rejection by the group meant death for our ancestors.

We protect our status and we work hard to build alliances because higher status means access to food, security and the opportunity to reproduce.

We demand our territory because it is there we feel safe to sleep and relax, because the territory provides us with a place where we can eat and rest at low risk.

Towards and Away Motivation

Today, powerful motives dominate business. We seek both to achieve objectives connected to these primal needs and to avoid losses that bring us closer to them.

Indeed, the instinct that many of us have to establish relationships at the cost of business results could be connected to the need to be accepted by others as the most important survival instinct. The ability to find food is less important than the value of remaining part of the group.

When it comes to decision making, we are much more inclined to reduce the risk of loss than to work towards goals.

Perhaps it is another hangover from the past that short-term fears were more significant than long-term goals, but nevertheless, there is much greater leverage through threatening to take something away than to offer something new.

A customer who has existing terms, perhaps a rebate for buying a certain volume of product, will react emotionally if that rebate is to be removed, even if they stand to gain more from a different contracting model.

A client I worked with wanted to restructure their partnerships with a large high-street retailer based on a higher percentage of online sales than in-store sales.

They proposed a shift of investment from paying for shop floor space in physical shops to paying for more space in the online world through advertising and communication.

Over time, the value of the investment would increase in line with the forecasted increase in sales, a point particularly notable because the current status was resulting in declining sales.

The retailer reacted very emotionally at the mention of the new structure, despite the additional value. Over the course of several years, the discussions became circular because the retailer would not accept the implied loss of investment.

I call the fear of loss away from motivation, and this away from motivation is an important driver of action.

Many people do not aspire to be the greatest; they simply hope to avoid failure. Their objective at work or academically is to pass tests and reach a safe place where they feel secure. The security of sitting in a group with the majority is enough.

This phenomenon can be noticed in aspects such as the uptake of new ideas and technology. Most people do not want to be early innovators, at the cutting edge; they just don't want to be left behind.

In marathon races such as the London Marathon that I have completed twice, the majority of entrants are not seeking to beat their best time or reach world-class standards. They are taking on the marathon as a physical and emotional challenge that they do not want to fail.

Others strive to be the best and are motivated by proving their excellence.

They constantly challenge themselves to improve, hit bigger goals, run faster, achieve more and prove to the world that they are excellent.

It is this second group I call towards motivated.

Undoubtedly, we are all a mixture of these two styles. In some aspects, we want to do our best and excel, while in others, we are satisfied with not failing.

It is overly simplistic to suggest that we are one or the other. When we are trying to influence other people, it is important to remember that a combination of proposals is more likely to have a greater impact.

When we make changes in life, such as getting fitter, losing weight, or earning more money, we instinctively map out a combination of goals.

We often start the process of change using a fear of failure.

It is said that the best time to discuss giving up smoking with a smoker is as they are recovering from their first heart attack.

The power of fear, the proximity of disaster and the realisation of what can be controlled become powerful motivators for change.

But away from motivation lasts only so long. Once the initial fear subsides and we reach a state of safety where the immediate risks are gone, the motivation fades.

At this point, towards motivation becomes an ally. Smokers might start for health reasons, but the accumulation of saved money and the prospect of holidays funded by the savings can be effective tools for continued abstinence.

The biggest risk in influence and motivation is the 'meh' part of the scale.

Many of us are inspired to act when we fear loss or failure, and many of us are persuaded to persevere by the allure of achievement and goals, but at times, especially in commercial relationships, there is not enough of either to be very influential.

When the people we are trying to influence are neither sufficiently worried about losing something, nor sufficiently inspired by the gains to make any changes, this is the 'meh' effect

Organisations such as Blockbuster, which are famous for their lack of adaptability and vision as the DVD rental market faded, did not change because their leadership did not fear the losses until it was too late, nor did they see significant rewards for change.

Change requires energy and resources. If the stress and energy required to change outweigh the value of the gains or are greater than the risk of doing nothing, then we are inclined to keep the status quo.

The present is familiar and safe, while change is uncertain. If its value appears small, then it is better and safer to keep things as they are, even if they are imperfect.

This is the 'meh' situation and is the biggest blocker of influence in commercial situations in my experience.

Game Theory

The film A Beautiful Mind is the story of John Nash, a talented mathematician plagued by mental illness. The film follows the life of Nash as he devises his theories of decision making and game theory called Nash Equilibrium, and at the same time, battles the debilitating effects of schizophrenia.

It is a powerful and inspiring portrayal of a man who faced the loneliness and darkness of mental illness while also developing cutting-edge theories that have been adopted by businesses around the world.

It is a movie that I watched before I understood the importance of game theory, and is the rare phenomenon of a Hollywood movie that captivates audiences on a dry topic such as mathematics. It was a precursor to The Imitation Game, a more recent portrayal of the ingenuity of Alan Turing during the Second World War to break the Enigma code, and after my discovery of the importance of John Nash in decision making, I simply had to revisit the film and watch it again.

Nash identified the mathematics and formulas behind a very simple human trait.

When faced with choices, in a situation with limited information, a lack of communication, and the addition of some competition or gains, humans resort to the 'least worst' option.

Counter to logic, we do not opt for the choice that will give us the biggest gains, nor do we choose the one that is most likely. We choose the option that is the safest.

One scenario used in game theory is to consider two people uncertain of their arrangements to meet. The options could be a restaurant preferred by one, the cinema preferred by the other or at home.

If they are unable to communicate and a choice of cinema, restaurant or home is required as a guess. They are both more likely to choose home, despite their preferences.

For either party, the choice of going home is less risky than the embarrassment and discomfort of being alone at the cinema or restaurant if the other person chooses a different option.

This is the Nash equilibrium, and I see it play out in business exercises I use during my workshops.

People make choices that are not ideal for their business but less risky for them personally, especially when discomfort and fear of loss are involved.

When faced with uncertainty, people are drawn to competitiveness, loss aversion, and suboptimal outcomes, as Nash predicted.

This phenomenon drives bidders to overpay for products during an auction. Rather than losing, they focus on the feeling of winning.

and their ego decides that paying more than they anticipated is better than losing, even if it is not the perfect outcome.

Game theory is used to influence decision-making through framing choices and is a powerful motivator.

Auctions are a prime example, but contracting within any competitive situation opens itself to the use of game theory and towards and away from motivation.

In certain markets, like France, retailers exclude one brand from their shelves each year, regardless of their public popularity. This exclusion drives a fear of failure and a hope of success that encourages sellers to bid more than necessary for a place, choosing the least worst outcome of overpaying rather than losing.

When faced with prices, we are often given three options: a high-cost version, a low-cost item, and a middle-cost item. Frequently, we choose the middle-cost item, and it is theorised that this choice is influenced by a balance of loss and gain.

Using Emotional Triggers.

Gain, loss, and the least-worst options are the foundations of influencing people, and they are enhanced when connected to our powerful emotional drivers in the chimp brain.

We all want things.

We want an increase in salary, new clothes, holidays, a nice home, a car, a promotion, and the opportunity to eat in nice restaurants.

When trying to influence someone, the question to explore is why they need these things. What emotional element does it serve for their chimp?

It is well understood that scarcity creates desire and will increase prices.

The sale of Oasis tickets in the UK and the amazing success of the Taylor Swift tour in 2024 both demonstrate how high demand for limited tickets drives up prices to extraordinary levels.

But this is a good example of how scarcity, a key strategy of influence, can satisfy several different desires of the chimp, and understanding which ones are driving people is essential in framing the scarcity in the most effective way.

Scarcity could create winners and losers. Winners get tickets, and losers do not. As such, someone who wants to be a winner and achieve success may want to buy a ticket because, by having one, they prove they are a winner. They might not be a fan of the music, but they are successful and resourceful enough to be able to buy one.

Scarcity can therefore also motivate people who fear missing out or losing.

They may not be able to deal with the fear that they are going to miss out on something that others will be enjoying. The high demand fuels their fears of missing out.

Some people might be passionate fans of the music, long-time listeners. The scarcity of the tickets drives them to buy, perhaps because they need to demonstrate consistency with their passion.

It would be unthinkable for a true fan, one known by everyone to be a supporter, to miss out on such a valuable experience.

In this case, they fear being inconsistent with previous actions and need to demonstrate through action that they are a true fan.

Still more people will want to attend the concert because they associate these scarce tickets with the elite, chosen or more important people in society. They want to be there to demonstrate to others that they are important enough to be able to get tickets.

Indeed, it is this last group who enjoy hospitality at sports events like Grand Prix races, tennis grand slam tournaments and football World Cup finals, despite having little or no interest in the sport at all.

When we understand that the same actions can be driven by different needs, it empowers us to frame proposals in more powerful ways to connect the items to the emotions more directly.

A proposal for the offer of concert tickets could be: Buy these tickets because the most important and high-status people are going. It could also be: Buy these tickets because if you don't, you will miss out on the event of the year. It could also be: I thought you were a massive supporter. Why would you not buy these tickets? They are a very special opportunity.

Difficult people are motivated by emotions. They are motivated towards goals, and they fear failure, just like everyone else.

Elon Musk is understood to be the wealthiest man in the world, yet I do not believe he is motivated by money.

If he were motivated by money, he has achieved more than he could have imagined and would stop pushing so hard, but he doesn't.

He pushed to take on the challenge of DOGE following the 2024 US presidential election, which would not add anything to his fortune. His association with the US president is costing him money, with a backlash against Tesla and the impact of tariff announcements.

So what motivates him?

I think Elon Musk is motivated to prove that he is the smartest person in the world and that he can do things that nobody else can or believes are possible.

It is absolutely incredible to watch one of the SpaceX rockets return to Earth and 'park' itself, especially given the technology in other rockets that causes them to crash back to Earth.

Returnable rockets, self-driving cars, the transformation to electric vehicles, and even slashing government expenditures are all challenges in the 'very hard to do' box, and Elon Musk is focused on all of them.

To motivate Elon Musk, simply present him with a challenge that others think is impossible. To inspire him to act, show him someone else who is smarter than he is and who delivers equally challenging projects.

Understanding & Delivering Value

In previous chapters, I shared the five elements of trust and how they are essential to delivering the balance of results and relationships that we seek.

Difficult people want to achieve goals, and to influence them, we must understand these goals and help them to achieve them.

The biggest difficulty in relationships with difficult people is likely to be not understanding or supporting their goals.

We focus on ourselves and want others to recognise what we need and help us.

We are able to achieve great things with people who share our goals; we struggle with those who do not.

But once you see beyond the specific goals and into the emotions driving these goals, you can see ways to deliver what they need.

A buyer who constantly demands the best prices, wants to price their worth to their leadership, or perhaps wants to prove they are strong and tough, or maybe they are chasing a bonus and the security and status money can bring.

What they are seeking is validation that they are doing a great job.

By agreeing to improved prices quickly, you are not helping them; you are creating a need to demand more. Their achievement comes when they work hard, challenge you, threaten you, and squeeze every penny. It is only through this journey that they can feel they have succeeded and evidence it to their leaders.

For this reason, you must resist, make it hard and have value that you are prepared to give away only when they demand it.

Opening with ambition is one of my key performance indicators for negotiation and delivers buyers exactly what they need when executed well.

Difficult people may be difficult because you do not understand them, their motives and fears, and you are not helping them succeed. That is where the trust is failing.

By taking steps to understand them more and to use emotional strategies to help them succeed, you unlock value.

Allow them to win, make them feel important, support their ego, encourage them to act in ways consistent with their statements and give them challenges to overcome.

But how can you understand what they need?

There are levels to explore, and I use a series of questions within preparation tools to help me with clients.

People want to deliver what they are measured on. First, find out what their measures are. What matters to them over the short and medium term? What is their manager tracking? These goals will be important to their success and will drive both towards motivation to hit them, and away from motivation if they are at risk.

What are their personal objectives? Do they want to get a promotion? If so, why? Are they seeking the security and value of increased salary and benefits, or are they chasing a more important position and greater status?

Are they someone who likes to drive nice cars, wear quality clothing, and go on expensive holidays?

Are they family-focused and work to support others around them?

These factors will tell you much about what their chimp demands.

Finally, explore the company they work for, the culture, their management, their goals and the future. These factors will drive what their leadership demands and tell you about external pressures they are under and the motives they are towards and away from in the wider business.

You can also learn much through their communication style, behaviours and actions.

Gather as much information as you can to formulate a profile of their towards goals, away from fears and some assumptions about the emotions that might be driving them.

When you talk to them and try to inspire change, it is essential that you create enough motivation to escape the 'meh' phase.

Be single-minded in your position and be as ambitious as possible. Unless you frame the opportunity as large enough or paint failure as significant enough, they might not be inspired to act.

Difficult people are chasing dreams and escaping nightmares. When you understand what these are, what their chimp needs to feel safe and what they are worried about, then you can choose topics wisely.

You support them with what is important, you avoid confrontation about their fears unless you are calculating them as leverage, and you empathise by adapting your behaviours.

A boss who is micromanaging you and disempowering you, as described earlier, might be afraid of looking bad to senior people if you make mistakes.

Rather than pushing them away, demanding space to work, bring them closer to you to witness your diligence and attention to detail, so that they learn to trust you.

You show them you know what they value, and you are delivering what they value, and they can rely on you.

When the moment is right, they will allow you to work without over scrutiny, or you have enough evidence to credibly have a difficult conversation with them, where you ask for that space based on your success.

TOUGH ON ISSUES, WARM ON PEOPLE

In 2025, Microsoft turned 50 years old and remains one of the largest and most successful companies of the modern era. Today, they are a leading light on the emerging technology of artificial intelligence (AI), and they continue to dominate the world of personal and business computing.

However, they have a checkered history and have been on the wrong end of Department of Justice judgments in the past.

An antitrust case brought against them during the 1990s found them to be acting unfairly. They were ordered to allow competition into their systems, a decision that resulted in the launch of new web browsers that were better and faster than Internet Explorer.

I heard a story recently about the previous CEO of Microsoft, Steve Ballmer, and his attitude to competition. He is a huge character with high energy, passion, and aggression. He initiated policies in the business to drive performance that force ranked every employee in every team and every project as projects were completed.

In every rating, there had to be at least one person rated as below expectations in his system. The result was a business entirely focused on politics, the protection of personal reputations and the avoidance of being the person singled out.

It became totally distracting and was a significant contributor to the failure of Microsoft to fulfil expectations during a transformational time for technology.

His attitude to external competition was equally aggressive as his treatment of internal colleagues.

He was openly aggressive and confrontational toward competitors such as Apple and hated their success. He rejected collaboration and cooperation and initiated a series of lawsuits against competitors, claiming theft of intellectual property.

He famously saw an intern walk into a meeting carrying an iPhone and lost his temper. He grabbed the device from the hands of the poor intern, humiliating them, before stamping on it in front of the audience.

Microsoft had failed to launch a successful smartphone, and the strategy to acquire Nokia did not go as planned.

Steve Ballmer was the CEO of one of the largest technology companies in the world, and they had failed to take advantage of the explosion of smartphones, the launch of cloud computing, social media and online shopping.

The day that Steve Ballmer resigned as CEO of the company the share price immediately rose by 7%, a damning judgment of his leadership.

He was a person who was obsessed with results at the expense of relationships. He cared little about the feelings of others as long as he got what he wanted. The downside of his approach was that the results did not deliver what they could have because he was not taking advantage of the richest resource he had available to him, the people around him.

Satya Nadella succeeded him as CEO. Satya Nadella holds a very different view of the balance of results and relationships. He recognises the power of people, their experiences and their knowledge to help everyone succeed.

He was instrumental in building a partnership with OpenAI that gave Microsoft access to technology that it could otherwise not have developed.

In 2019, he made an investment in OpenAI. They were a not-for-profit organisation performing cutting-edge research into the development of large language models and generative AI technology.

They were widely regarded to be leading the way with their innovations, and contrary to the previous leadership, Satya Nadella chose to build bridges, not try to create walls.

His investments helped OpenAI accelerate its technology development and gave Microsoft access to incorporate this innovative and transformative technology into its systems before anyone else.

He recognises that technology, software, and hardware are all connected and highly complex. He sees the interdependencies on development, manufacturing and supply with companies like Apple, Sony and Samsung all competitors in the finished smartphone market, but all of which participate in supplying technology and parts to each other in their manufacture.

Building walls and initiating lawsuits in an environment so interdependent damaged Microsoft, cutting them off from important developments.

Today, they are a burgeoning business. They transformed their suite of Microsoft Office tools into online software as a service applications available across all devices, including Apple. They have led the way in AI through the partnership with OpenAI, and they are exploring imaginative new partnerships to find technology solutions to problems around the world.

Satya Nadella is not simply people-focused. He is performance and business-focused, but he understands the value of people in the equation.

People are more than a means to an end; they are expendable and replaceable.

They create a culture, bring knowledge, have ideas, support each other and collaborate to unlock more than could be expected.

If you want to go fast, go alone, but if you want to go far, go together.

This mantra echoes through every part of human performance because we are built as communities of people who cooperate to deliver magic.

Difficult people are not there to sabotage ideas and destroy results. They simply see the way forward differently from you and others.

At times, they have lost the balance between results and relationships, perhaps because they only see that path, or perhaps because, under pressure, we default to a task-first approach.

Understanding them, their motives, their beliefs, and their attitudes can unlock value for you. If you can find enough trust to get things done when others cannot, you have given yourself an advantage.

Satya Nadella was not new to Microsoft. For many years, he worked in the business under Steve Ballmer, and he survived and thrived enough to build a reputation to be in contention for the top job, and he did so with a very different approach to people.

The balance of results and relationships starts with results.

It is your responsibility to deliver for yourself and for the business; that is how you create the security you need to be safe and get the recognition you need to develop.

But if your focus is solely on results, then you will damage the performance culture you need to thrive.

Your emphasis is to be tough on tasks, but warm on relationships.

Separate the task from the people.

It is possible and even desirable to have a challenging conversation with a colleague or a customer and to disagree about the terms of a deal, and then afterwards go for a drink and dinner.

When you respect that someone is doing their job to get the best terms they can and they are not acting to personally damage you, then it is easy to make this distinction.

A change of language will make a huge difference.

Instead of being rejecting, responding, "no, no, no" to their proposals and ideas be positive. "Thank you for the suggestions, let's keep discussing until we find something that does work"

Use questions, not to challenge and take power, but to be curious and understand.

Questions that demand 'why?' and 'what were you thinking?' Or "how do you think I could even consider that" are not questions; they are challenges.

Questions loaded with "tell me more," "that's interesting, what triggered that?' And "can you give me more details?" are curious and can open up discussions.

These questions give insight, information and build trust. Challenging questions close down conversation, impose authority, and increase tension and conflict.

When you are warm with people, you are curious, positive and calm. You also use reciprocity to encourage cooperation.

By demonstrating some willingness, taking a small risk, sharing some information and offering something, you create an atmosphere where they are encouraged to do the same.

It shows vulnerability and humility, traits that are powerful assets when you are solving problems with difficult people at work.

Difficult people are only so from our point of view. Perhaps we are the problem?

By adopting the ideas in this book, you have a much greater opportunity to understand what it is that they are doing that makes them feel difficult to you.

They enable you to take steps to change. You can have the courage to have difficult conversations that are clear, balanced and calm. You can explore the trust you have and the trust you want, and you can address issues of the imbalance between results and relationships that so often cause the problems.

Many of the personalities in this book are difficult because they are self-oriented and results-focused.

They are often difficult because they do not care about people.

For exactly this reason, you must embrace discomfort, find the right moment, and address the situation.

When you do, by being tough on task but warm on people, you are likely to build respect, draw boundaries and unlock opportunities that were there all along.

Steve Ballmer was one of the early team members of Microsoft and instrumental in its success. He made a lot of money and is famous around the world.

However, for me, he will be the CEO who almost broke one of the most successful companies on earth by obsessing over winning and undervaluing partnerships and people.

He missed all the major transformations in technology during the late 2000s, and that says everything I need to know about people obsessed with winning and who do not care about the power of people.

THE SECRET TO GETTING THE ELEPHANT OUT OF THE ROOM

I came up with the title of the book after thinking about what it means to be sitting across the table from a difficult manager, difficult colleague or difficult customer.

It conjured up the image of the elephant in the room in my mind, and I recognised that what we really want in this situation is to be able to deal with the elephant. We want to be able to bring up the difficulties in the relationship and address problems one by one calmly and thoughtfully.

We usually don't do that because we fear how they will react and expect them to react emotionally, deny the problem exists at all, blame us for the problem, or perhaps all three.

Instead, we sit in the room and hope something gets better, allowing the elephant to sit there too, getting in the way of productive business relationships.

If you expected to read through this book and identify a series of simple tips and tricks through which you could transform circumstances with the difficult people around you, I can imagine that you are feeling disappointed because clearly, that is not how this book works.

The difficult people around us come in many forms, some of whom I have described in this book, but there are many others whom I have not mentioned.

They are difficult because they think, feel and believe differently from you. That is the essence of the problem.

There are many articles online describing the behaviour and the frustrations caused by micro-managers.

During my professional engagements, it is one of the most complained-about issues. People hate being micromanaged.

In this book, I described them as disempowering. We explored their fear of mistakes. We discussed that they take pride in doing a great job and being successful, and that is the heart of their motivation.

The fact is that not a single manager reads an article about micro-management and recognises themselves in the descriptions.

They have no idea that their actions are micro-management.

As far as they are concerned, they are setting high standards and tracking performance to ensure they are met.

In fact, during the writing of this book, I spoke with a client on this very subject.

She explained that she wants to develop more patience with people who complain and aren't achieving her high standards.

I would guess that if I asked her team, they would agree that she is impatient, demanding too much, and micro-managing.

The question is, who gets to decide whether someone is difficult or not?

This question sits at the heart of the problem because when we notice that there is a problem, both sides are ready and willing to blame the other and call them difficult.

After reading this book, you will realise that spotting the difficulties puts you in a stronger position because you now have the power to do something about them.

The way to outsmart difficult people at work is not to find manipulative ways to get them to change and operate the way that you want them to, because they are unlikely to ever do so.

The way to outsmart them is to recognise that you have a problem and decide that the relationship is important enough to want to repair the situation.

Once you have made this powerful choice, you are demonstrating humility, which is what you need to ultimately find the value that you are seeking.

Difficult people are unlikely to change because they do not know they are difficult.

They start with positive intentions. They have goals and they have ways of working that have probably served them well for many years, and so they use them.

The difficulty is that these working methods do not help you succeed.

You need humility to accept that you are the one who will have to change to improve things.

Your power comes from understanding that changing to reduce friction with them will unlock additional value for yourself. You will also learn much about your ability to adapt to different circumstances and different people. These skills will serve you well for many years because difficult people are everywhere.

Once you know there is a problem and you have decided to take control and empower yourself to outsmart them, the easier part comes.

Exploring what is important to them, what motivates them and what emotional recognition they need.

Micromanagers fear failure and probably fear being unprepared for conversations with their leadership. Knowing every detail helps them feel confident.

They lack trust in the team.

To succeed, you need to bring them closer, not push them away.

Prove to them that they are able to trust you, your delivery and your expertise. Once you achieve this, they will allow you to help them look good.

Demanding buyers want to show they deliver great value. By pushing you, they prove they are valuable.

When you expect it, anticipate it, and embrace it, you can make proposals that allow them to get concessions, but only the ones you have planned.

You let them win, so that you can win.

With difficult, negative colleagues, they are trying to demonstrate that they are thinkers and prepared for the worst.

They want to anticipate problems and get credit for helping the team avoid disaster.

Perhaps they have a point, and including them at the right moment could help with preparation.

A great business requires people with different ideas and different ways of thinking.

Difficult people are assets. They stop you from working in groups that all think the same way. They enrich your preparation and force you to think in new ways.

When you take time to recognise a positive intention and reflect on what emotions are driving their actions, you become able to deliver that for them and at the same time create more robust business results.

However, you must recognise that the elephant will sit there unless you address some behaviours and communicate better.

You cannot simply accommodate difficult people and expect results. That is focusing too much on relationships and forgetting results.

Leaders have two responsibilities in this regard.

First, they must get the most from each person in the group. Recognising their strengths and differing skills and avoiding judging them for being difficult if they do not conform.

Second, they have a responsibility to the group to ensure a great result and a positive atmosphere. They cannot allow the behaviour of one to damage the morale and atmosphere for all.

Getting the elephant out of the room requires you to recognise the problem, be humble enough to accept that you are going to fix it and have to change, invest time reflecting on what their motives are and finally be prepared to have difficult conversations and risk the relationship.

Trust is fundamental, and when there is a difficult person, there is a gap in trust.

They may not be giving you the value you need. Perhaps they do not know what is important to you. It could be that they haven't shown themselves to be credible or empowered enough, or maybe they are unreliable. Finally, perhaps they are just unwilling to admit failings and flaws.

Any one or any combination of these aspects is likely to be the diagnosis of the problem.

Combined with the power of trying to think and feel the way they do and the courage to have difficult conversations when needed, you can outsmart difficult people.

The elephant will not jump up and walk out of the room. But they will go when you spot it, understand why they are there and take action to get them to move.

I hope this book has helped you to understand why certain people are difficult. I hope that you feel able to understand their motives and you have the courage to adapt in order to overcome their challenges.

Looking back at the surgeon from The Royal Glamorgan Hospital, I know that today I would behave very differently.

I am convinced today that if I asked him, he would have told me how disrespectful I was. I am sure that he would describe me as difficult.

That is the point.

Difficulty lies on both sides. If you think they are difficult, they think you are difficult.

It is up to you to find a way to solve this problem, and that is likely to mean you are the one who needs to be more understanding and change.

Looking back at my time as a young representative in Wales with the surgeon, today I can identify a problem that we both shared. Perhaps that was the place to focus my efforts?

The real problem we had in the area was not which drug he chose to use, but the lack of confidence in general practice to diagnose and treat the disease in the first place, plus the lack of willingness of men to come forward with symptoms until it was too late.

I wonder if we had worked together on these shared problems, perhaps we would have found a way to work closely together.

Doing so would have helped me to grow my sales and helped his department to treat more people in need.

We could have created a strong alliance instead of me feeling furious, disappointed and humiliated.

This insight is worth considering. Outsmarting difficult people requires thinking about the true goal rather than winning the conflict. You must also have the humility, understanding, and courage to earn respect and unlock real value—let them have the ego, and focus on the results.

If you asked them, they would tell you that you are the difficult one.

They are likely to see that there is a problem; the difference is that, after reading this book, you want to do something about it.

Telling them they are difficult isn't going to work.

You need to see that 'there is difficulty' and choose to fix it.

You need to be clear about what you want, and then seek strategies, behaviours and actions that create that situation.

That means controlling your emotions, not blaming them for being difficult, and taking steps to build trust through a combination of difficult conversations, empathy, and thoughtful action.

CHECKLISTS TO GET THE ELEPHANT OUT OF THE ROOM

I am a strong advocate of checklists. I use them daily to manage my tasks and guide the structure of workshops and events I deliver with clients.

They are the secret tool that appears again and again when I talk to experts who operate in high-pressure environments.

As a sportsman, I have seen their use in everything from nutrition planning to team warm-ups.

I have talked to doctors who use them in preparation for surgery to ensure the correct processes and resources are used to avoid mistakes, and I know that they are used in the military and aviation to ensure consistency and excellence.

They are simple, effective and powerful, yet remain underused in business.

We have a temptation to avoid simple solutions, perhaps because we feel that we are beyond such simplicity. We seem to baulk at the idea of following a process and system, perhaps because we fear impact on creativity. We seem to avoid repetitive tasks and automation because we seem to want to add our personal mark on each day.

All of these reasons are connected to emotional barriers such as the need for recognition, status, respect for our creativity and the need to feel empowered and independent.

A refusal to embrace the power of checklists could be enough to make you a difficult person in the eyes of your manager, your customer or your colleagues.

There are powerful justifications for the importance of checklists.

They reduce errors because you don't need to remember the details of every task, freeing you up to think about more important subjects.

They create consistency, ensuring that excellence becomes the standard.

They ensure accountability, keeping track of who completed which task and when.

When partnered with a robust review process that explores each major event and identifies areas of development and improvement, they simplify and accelerate results.

Their use in high-performance sports, medicine, aviation, and the military attests to their importance and contribution to the consistency of results.

These are examples that inspire books, leaders, businesses and programmes around the world and deserve to be learned from.

In the spirit of checklists as a critical tool for results, I have shared some checklists that will help you to overcome difficult people at work and get the elephant out of the room.

They cover preparing for difficult conversations, gathering information about key people in order to better understand their motivations and fears, building effective proposals and some questions that will help you to explore issues of trust across a team.

They each provide questions for reflection or points of planning that take you through the mental journey required to succeed with difficult people.

Preparing for Difficult Conversations.

The goal of this tool is to help you prepare for a difficult conversation, consider points you want to raise, but also to anticipate reactions, so you are ready to deal with different responses.

- [ ] What is the goal of the conversation? Are you clear about what you want them to say or do as a result of the meeting? Be specific.

- [ ] Do you have evidence to support your points? Be clear about what they said and did, and their effect.

- [ ] How did they make you feel? e.g. do not say, you were disrespectful; instead, say I felt disrespected. They are unlikely to have intended to act that way, and accusations will lead to an argument about intent, not effect.

- [ ] How will you set the scene? What will you say or do that prepares them to have this type of discussion?

- [ ] Write the statement you want to make. Keep it clear and precise to communicate the message. Do not try to soften the effect; it might lead to misunderstanding.

- [ ] Practice the statement by reading it aloud. Become comfortable with the words.

- [ ] Support the statement with your evidence. Keep it precise and focused. Use one example to start with.

- [ ] Consider their reaction. How will they feel? Surprised, offended, threatened, challenged, disbelieving, other?

- [ ] What statements might they use to defend themselves or argue with your position?

- [ ] What questions might they ask for clarification or supporting evidence?

- [ ] What threats might they make, defensive actions or escalations?

- [ ] How are you going to avoid an argument? Practice using silence to reduce tension.

- [ ] Practice your proposal on how to resolve the difficulty. Write out ideas.

- [ ] Consider if you want to make suggestions and discuss, or make statements, they must follow, or share ideas and listen.

- [ ] How will you conclude the conversation amicably? e.g. thank you for listening, and I would like to discuss this more when we have had a chance to think about it. Or, we aren't going to resolve this now, but I appreciate you talking to me. Can we talk again in the future?

- [ ] How will you follow up, an email, a phone call, or a message?

- [ ] What are your next steps and schedule?

Understanding Needs and Motives

As we have seen, clashes between difficult people and us often result from misunderstandings of intention or miscommunication.

When we learn what really motivates people, we can start to understand why tension exists.

In a meeting with a client, I ran a trust and understanding exercise. A response from one team member on their proudest achievement in life was to explain that they came from being a technician to a senior person, and they never expected it.

Later, there was discussion about goals and responsibilities. This person was very defensive about why one of their key priorities was an objective for a colleague, and he was angry.

To me, it was obvious why.

He perhaps felt that he was not being respected and recognised for his expertise and was, in essence, being pushed lower in the hierarchy. This feeling was counter to his greatest achievement and undermined his identity.

No wonder he was angry.

This tool is designed to help you explore the goals and motives of people, covering their business goals, personal goals, organisation priorities and their ways of working. All these factors will be important elements in driving their behaviour and will affect their emotions. These are the factors that will make them difficult on certain topics.

Personal Objectives

- ☐ What are their specific targets and goals?
- ☐ How do they measure success?
- ☐ What metrics or KPIs are important to them?
- ☐ What are their long-term personal aspirations?
- ☐ What concerns or challenges do they face?

Business Culture

- ☐ What are the primary business objectives of the organisation?
- ☐ What core values drive their business decisions?
- ☐ How does the organisation typically operate?
- ☐ What are their standard processes and workflows?
- ☐ How does the organisation approach risk?
- ☐ Are they risk-averse or risk-tolerant?
- ☐ How quickly does the organisation adapt to change?

Personal Beliefs

- ☐ What is the nature of their relationships within their organisation and with external partners?
- ☐ How do they view authority and hierarchy within their organisation?

- ☐ How do they handle conflict?

- ☐ Are they confrontational or more diplomatic?

- ☐ What is their preferred communication style?

- ☐ Are they direct or indirect?

- ☐ What personal values are important to them?

Building Impactful Proposals

There is a recipe for building effective proposals. When people are evaluating ideas, they have certain criteria that matter to them.

This checklist enables you to consider all the elements that are essential and include them in a structure that can quickly be adapted to various media, including presentations, documents, slides and conversations.

To add impact, proposals need to be connected to influencing feelings and come to life through stories, and these can easily be incorporated into the model.

- ☐ Describe the current situation and the problem that you are trying to solve.

- ☐ Develop a story that perfectly illustrates the problem through human eyes.

- ☐ Summarise your idea or solution into a paragraph that is easily remembered. This is the easy-to-remember solution that you need them to be able to quickly repeat to colleagues when asked what the solution is.

☐ Create a story that describes how your solution will solve the problem for the audience and what the new solution will look and feel like.

☐ Explain the details of how and why your solution works. Include technical data as necessary to support the argument with evidence.

☐ Describe the specific benefits of adopting your proposal to the decision maker. They are concerned with their personal agenda and want to know what is in it for them.

☐ Define the steps required to adopt and implement the solution to illustrate you know how to execute and have considered the details.

Assessing and Building Trust in Teams

We have a relationship with the team we are on, and it is different from the relationships we have with the individuals.

It is possible to have a group of people who have strong relationships with each other but who do not function well as a group.

Equally, it is possible to have a group that does not get along well but who makes an excellent team.

What matters is how the individuals relate to the group as a whole. This checklist helps to explore the individual's relationship with the group and can uncover opportunities to improve and differences that can be resolved.

Encourage individuals to answer questions themselves and discuss answers.

A more in-depth workshop is available and works effectively with clients. These questions are a helpful illustration and starting point for leaders who want to explore issues without help.

The same model works for customer relationships. Buyers and sellers who work together over long periods need trust to work effectively together. Considering these questions in the context of the business relationship provides insight into areas where issues exist and presents opportunities for solutions.

Personal Reflection – Shared Value

- [ ] Describe what tangible and intangible rewards you would like to receive from being part of this group. Be honest and be specific. Emphasise intangible rewards as these are more powerful and more regular.

- [ ] How would you like to be seen by others who look at your work within this group?

- [ ] How would you like them to describe you to your manager?

- [ ] What actions can the people in this group take to help you achieve the rewards you described above?

- [ ] Focus on the next 60 days. What steps could you take to feel more rewarded for your effort?

Personal Reflection – Deep Understanding.

- [ ] What are your biggest priorities in life?

- [ ] What do you look forward to?

☐ What motivates you?

☐ What excites you?

☐ What goals do you have personally or professionally over the next few years?

☐ What worries you at work or at home?

☐ What achievement are you most proud of in work or in your life?

☐ What do you dislike in the world?

☐ What types of people frustrate you?

☐ Are there specific behaviours and actions that you don't approve of in the world?

☐ How would you like other people to describe you after meeting you for the first time?

Personal Reflection – Credibility

☐ Do you feel that the group believes in the high standard of your skills?

☐ What would you like to see and hear from them to demonstrate that they judge you to be an expert?

☐ Do you feel empowered to deliver on your tasks?

☐ What could be done to help you feel more able to deliver what you need to do without interference, so that you feel trusted, empowered and credible in the group?

Personal Reflection – Reliability

☐ Does the team deliver on its promises to you?

☐ Does it meet its deadlines so that you can deliver what you need in a timely way?

☐ What is your expectation when someone in the team promises that something will be done? How confident are you that they will keep their word?

☐ What steps could be taken to increase your confidence in the team's reliability in delivering on promises?

Personal Reflection – Vulnerability

☐ What would happen if you asked someone for help on something that you 'should' know? How would that feel?

☐ Would you be prepared to openly question others in the group without fear of consequences later?

☐ Are you prepared to suggest ideas that are unusual without fear of judgment?

☐ When was the last time you admitted to this group that you were wrong and had made a mistake?

☐ When you are with this group, are you cautious about what you say and do in case you are judged negatively?

☐ What actions can be taken by the group to increase the feelings of safety?

☐ Are there examples you can remember of when something happened that reduced the feelings of safety and made you aware of the need to be cautious?

ABOUT THE AUTHOR

Christopher Webber is a renowned expert in business performance, specialising in succeeding with difficult customers.

As the founder of Foxleigh Commercial Performance, Chris has dedicated his career to empowering clients with the skills and strategies needed to enhance revenue, drive productivity, and build strong partnerships. His unique approach emphasises effective communication and trust-building, even in the most challenging situations.

Chris began his professional life at 18 as a rugby league player for Wigan before transitioning into sales and commercial roles. He has a background in consulting and leadership roles at prestigious organisations like The Gap Partnership and GSK. Chris has unique experiences in high-performance sport, sales, negotiation, and strategic planning.

His work spans various industries, including pharmaceuticals, healthcare, manufacturing, fast-moving consumer goods and transport, where he has successfully driven significant commercial growth and business performance.

Chris has established himself as a thought leader and is in demand by organisations around the world to help them overcome significant business challenges when they need it the most.

For more information about how he can help you outsmart difficult people at work, visit www.foxleigh.net.

ACKNOWLEDGEMENTS

Dozens of people have helped me produce this book, and it would be impossible to thank them all, especially since many of them were the difficult individuals who helped me learn, evolve, and develop my skills. Thank you to the people I have met in my career who challenged me and with whom I struggled to connect fully. It is because of those experiences that I have become the person I am today and was able to write this book.

My sincerest thanks must go to Graham Drew, who diligently read early versions of the text and offered his detailed and highly considered advice to help shape the final version. His attention to detail, thoughtfulness and insight were invaluable, and his support and guidance as a colleague and friend have been essential for many years.

Thanks also to David Ford, Tim Kemp, Linda Stephens, Matt Rogers, Helen Lynch, Samantha Ferry, Rod Muir, Jose Aguilar, Kieran Kelly and Mary Corrie who took the time to read and offer thoughtful and valuable feedback. Without your positive words of encouragement and dedication to reading, the book may not have been published. It was your support that gave me the confidence to continue.

Thank you to all the people who offered to read and provide feedback. I was overwhelmed by the reaction from people whom I had never met, or who were old connections and contacts, but who were willing to offer support and advice. There was a moment after I finished the book when I wondered if anyone would be interested in reading it. The reaction I received from all of you convinced me that the answer is yes.

Thank you to Abigail Baldwin and the team at Buttercrumble for the design and layout of the book. Their creativity and imagination were inspiring, and they were patient and flexible enough to accommodate my whims and indecision.

A special thanks to Maria Louis for her unwavering support and inspiration. Her passion and confidence with all things performance have inspired me to explore new ways to engage and connect with people. The podcast, live podcast events, Foxleigh workshops, and my presentation style have all benefited from her willingness to say yes to new ideas and her high standards of production, which have constantly driven me towards excellence.

Finally, I would like to thank my family for their constant support and love. They each inspire me every day with their courage to be themselves and pursue their passions. They have encouraged me to follow my dreams and to be more "Chris", as they are each 100% themselves.

Without their shining lights, fun, excitement and patience, life would be incomplete.